I

INTRODUCTION
Ellen Lupton

4

PRELUDE
THE AVANT-GARDE TRAJECTORY
Monica Strauss

8

REFERENCE POINTS
DESIGN IN THE NETHERLANDS SINCE 1945
William Deere

14

NON-LINING FIGURES
ON RECENT DUTCH TYPE DESIGN
Robin Kinross

22

THE END OF HOUSE STYLE?
A GRAPHIC DESIGN PROJECT AT
THE CENTRAAL MUSEUM, UTRECHT
Daan de Kuyper

33

GRAPHIC DESIGN IN THE NETHERLANDS
A SELECTION OF RECENT WORK

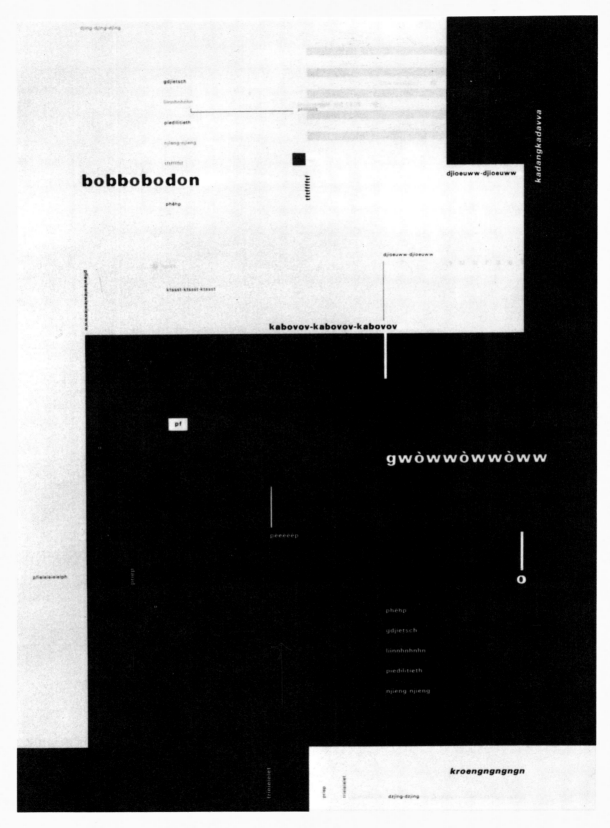

Back side of letter paper designed by
Berry van Gerwen. The purplish black printing
is intended to show through on the front side
of the paper.

factuur   datum ●

INTRODUCTION

This book accompanies an exhibition of recent work by emerging Dutch designers; because the high-profile studios of the 1980s have been well-covered in the American press, the curators chose to present new work which has not been seen much outside the Netherlands. The young, independent figures featured in this project are making their way in a culture which is exceptionally hospitable towards design. Holland has a long history of artistic invention, religious and political tolerance, and active engagement in the development of modern publishing; more recently, the alliance of Holland's largely socialized public sphere with its prosperous private sector has nurtured a profound care for the visual environment that is perhaps unmatched by any other Western country. The government is a major supporter of design, through grants for experimental work and through contracts for government publications—it is more common to think of such agencies in the Netherlands as "commissioners" than "clients," rather as one would describe a patron of the fine arts in the US. The Netherlands' remarkable public commitment to design (together with the persistent sales efforts of designers) has encouraged private institutions to employ challenging graphics in their house styles and publications as well, yielding a visual landscape that is as varied as the land is flat.

*Front side of letter paper designed by
Berry van Gerwen.*

The work of emerging Dutch designers is produced in the context of recent developments in Dutch graphics and the older trajectory of modernism. In her essay, Monica Strauss surveys the historic avant-garde, culminating with the career of Willem Sandberg, whose love of cheap, left-over materials continues to inform Dutch graphic design. William Deere charts the rise and fall of rational modernism in the post-WWII period, from the minimalist logic of Total Design to the reactive expressionism of Studio Dumbar and Hard Werken. Robin Kinross connects recent type design to the tradition of twentieth-century Dutch typography, revealing a continuity between the most outrageous experiments of the emerging generation and the philosophy and craftsmanship of their teachers. Daan de Kuyper's essay "The End of House Style?" is a case study written from a *client's* point of view: De Kuyper describes the institutional identity (or non-identity) commissioned by the Centraal Museum in Utrecht in 1990, a project whose experimental engagement with graphic design is anathema to most American museums, which tend to treat designers as the generic "suppliers" of a necessary but intrinsically secondary service.

What is "Dutch design"? In the process of creating this publication and its sibling exhibition, the words and ideas of two great designers have repeatedly come to mind: Gert Dumbar and Jan van Toorn. These mature figures are not the focus of this project, yet their impact on contemporary design resonates through the graphics shown in this book. In a conversation with Gert Dumbar in The Hague in September 1991, he argued that the secret of Dutch design lies in the culture's unique commitment to individualism and its spontaneous sense of humor—its ability to take itself not *too* seriously. He warned us against presenting so-called "Dutch design" (which is quickly entering American journalism as the banner of a new style) as a ready-made code available for instant quotation.

Second page of letter paper designed by Harmine Louwé, Studio Dumbar, for Atlas Venture, a Dutch bank.

2

Staalstraat 13a
1011 JK Amsterdam
telefoon 020 20 39 80

boekhandel en antiquariaat

Nijhof ———— Lee

&

"Americans," Dumbar cautioned, "want to make stable myths out of phenomena that are still in flux, such as 'Dutch design.' But our attitude is more clever than the American talent for manufacturing myths. In the end we [the Dutch] will escape the myth."

Jan van Toorn is less sanguine about Dutch individualism; he notes a lack of critical consciousness among the country's graphic designers, whose visually rigorous yet intellectually single-minded educations encourage an interest in form above all else. With a few exceptions—notably the work of Linda van Deursen and Armand Mevis—the work presented in this publication is primarily concerned with inventing unique formal languages, from the exquisitely rigorous concepts of Irma Boom to the personalized graphic signatures of Berry van Gerwen and Harmine Louwé. In a conversation with Jan van Toorn in New York, October 1991, he commented, "Holland is the perfect example of repressive tolerance. There is no interest there in the ideological basis of anything—whether it's design or politics. The Dutch have been too busy keeping their feet dry to worry about ideology."

In response to these conflicting mandates from two heroes of Holland, this publication modestly presents some artifacts designed in The Netherlands; we offer them not as evidence of a coherent style, but as the traces of individual sensibilities formed within a specific culture. If there were any feature of "Dutch design" we might wish to import to North America, it would not be its peculiar stylistic mannerisms, but rather the nation's impressive commitment to visual research. Perhaps the next generation of designers in The Netherlands will take up Van Toorn's proposal to study the relations between the individual producer and "the social conditions which determine the formation of public discourse."[1]

E.L.

Rabobank 39.38.11.980   postgiro 5914454   K.v.K. 201.681

Letter paper designed by Frits Deys,
for an antiquarian book shop.

1. Jan van Toorn, *Policy 1993–1996, Institute for Fine Arts, Design, and Theory* (Maastricht: Jan van Eyck Academy, 1991) 7.

Page from Experimenta Typographica,
designed by Willem Sandberg, 1967.

PRELUDE:
THE AVANT-GARDE TRAJECTORY IN HOLLAND
Monica Strauss

The revolution in typography and graphic design that occurred between the wars was a direct result of the interest of avant-garde artists in design issues. The Italian Futurists, as early as 1912, and the Dada artists, beginning in 1917, attacked typographic conventions and, as a revolutionary gesture, introduced unorthodox layouts and arbitrary combinations of letterforms in their publications. After World War I, the new avant-garde—members of the Bauhaus, De Stijl and Constructivism—saw that design and typography, now liberated from earlier constraints, could be reconstructed to reflect their own thoughts on the role of art in the industrial age.

Calling their approach to design "The New Typography," artists such as Kurt Schwitters, El Lissitzky, and Moholy-Nagy turned to advertising to demonstrate what they called a machine aesthetic. Traditional ornament was rejected, as was any evidence of the artist's hand in the form of drawing, woodcut, or etching. The advertiser's message was to be presented as legibly as possible by using sans serif type, the ornaments available in the type case, photographic illustrations, and primary colors. Visual interest was to be achieved through asymmetrical compositions, in which letterforms, illustrations, and the open spaces of the page played an equal role.

In all this ferment, the Dutch were very much in the vanguard, thanks to the pioneering work of the architect/designer Piet Zwart (1885-1977). Like many great innovators, Zwart was an amateur. He studied art and architecture, and in the early 20s he served as an assistant to the architect Jan Wils, a member of De Stijl. When Wils began to receive commissions for graphic design projects, he encouraged Zwart to enter the field. As Zwart recalls, "I started out without the slightest idea of what typography was. I didn't even know the meaning of the terms upper and lower case."

Zwart's earliest attempts reflected the horizontal and vertical orientation of De Stijl, but by the time he came to design the landmark 80-page Netherlands Cable Catalogue, published in Dutch and English in 1928, he had created his own form of the New Typography. Zwart, who composed his pages with architectural precision, insisted on doing his own photography and writing his own material. This allowed him to express a Dada sense of play in verbal and visual puns, witty slogans, expressive lettering, and whimsical parallels between word and picture. His originality lay

Advertisement designed by Vilmar Huszar, 1917.

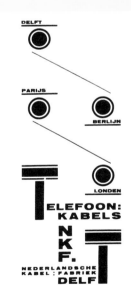

Advertisement designed by Piet Zwart, c.1924.

Logo designed by Piet Zwart, c.1921.

5

in combining this lightness of approach with the strictest principles of Constructivist composition. Layouts with a strong spatial thrust on the diagonal joined photographs, photomontages, letterforms, rules, and discs into a dynamic whole.

Surprisingly, Zwart had only two committed disciples in the 20s: Paul Schuitema (1897-1973) and Gerard Kiljan (1891- 1968). Schuitema, who also learned to do his own photography, had a more direct, less playful approach than Zwart. His layouts had the classical simplicity of the De Stijl compositions of both Mondrian and Van Doesburg. In his advertisements for Berkel Company, he used flat discs or squares of color to set off the hard-edge photographs of scales and slicing machines, giving these mundane objects a monumental presence. These strong images were balanced by the strict justification of the texts, so that the groupings of words functioned as yet another geometric element, but in a lighter way.

Gerard Kiljan also produced advertisements and brochures according to the tenets of the New Typography. His great contribution, however, was the establishment of a graphic design course at the Hague Academy in the early 30s, that was inspired by Zwart's innovations. Up to that time, Zwart's impact had been negligible. In reviewing the yearbook of applied art published in 1927, Zwart complained that not one example illustrated there reflected the "fresh young spirit" of the modern world. Once his ideas were integrated into a school curriculum, however, a whole group of young designers, including Dick Elffers, Wim Brusse, Cas Oorthuys, and Henny Cahn began to follow his lead.

Nevertheless, by the end of the 30s a rebellion against a system which excluded so many other approaches to design began to be felt. The younger generation urged a loosening of the tenets of the machine aesthetic, in order to include a greater variety of typefaces, to experiment with graphic media other than photography, and to unlock the rigidity of the compositional grid.

Advertisement designed by Gerard Kiljan, 1927.

Advertisement designed by Paul Schuitema, c.1928.

The designer who bridged the gap between the generations and who laid the foundations for postwar Dutch graphic design was Willem Sandberg (1897-1894). Sandberg, twelve years younger than Zwart, was initially trained as an artist, but after dabbling in psychology and various healing cults, he moved into the field of pictorial statistics and graphic design in the 1930s. With his diversified background, powerful opinions, and strong personality, Sandberg soon became a person to be reckoned with in Amsterdam art circles. He was often called upon to advise the Stedelijk Museum on exhibitions, and, in 1936, he was named its director and chief curator.

In the 1930s Surrealism began to supersede Constructivism as the dominant artistic influence on design. Free organic compositions now seemed more appropriate to an aesthetic philosophy that emphasized the inner life rather than the outer world. Although Sandberg's designs of the 30s still rely on photographs, the images are often set against soft, cloud-like forms and are combined with cursive typefaces or letters of his own design.

In 1942, because of his underground activities against the Nazis, Sandberg was forced into hiding. However, even during the fifteen months he lived in the small southern town of Gennep under the assumed name of Henri Willem van der Bosch, he continued to design by compiling pamphlets written and illustrated by hand. The shortage of materials had a lasting influence on Sandberg's aesthetic. As he wrote, "I don't like luxury in the use of typography, the use of gold or brilliant paper. I prefer the rough in contour and surface, torn forms and wrapping papers."

The long series of catalogues and posters produced by Sandberg for the Stedelijk Museum between the end of the war and the 70s proved to be a brilliant synthesis of the ideals of the New Typography and the expressive freedom encouraged by Surrealism and the inevitable compromises of wartime. Sandberg's clear, simple compositions and almost exclusive use of primary colors were rooted in the experiments of the 20s. What he added were his characteristic torn-paper letterforms, cursive type, mottled inking, textured papers, primitive figuration, and a collage-like layering of form. Legibility and clarity remained the ideal, but the hand of the individual was no longer denied.

It is from this foundation that contemporary Dutch design springs.

Cover designs by Willem Sandberg, 1946.

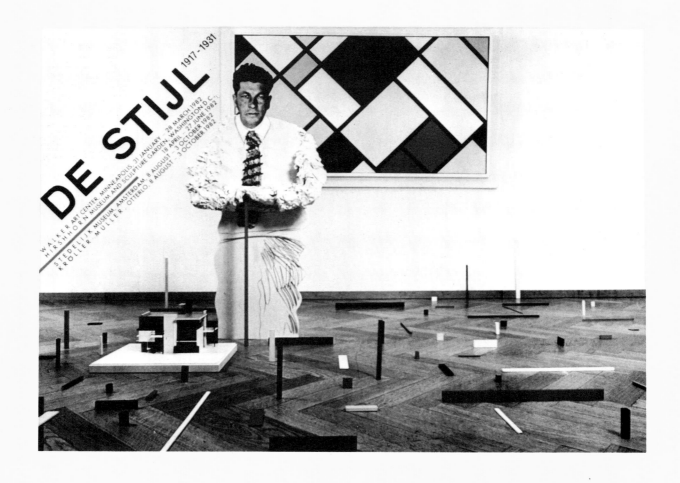

Poster designed by Gert Dumbar/
Studio Dumbar, 1982. Photography
by Lex van Pieterson.

Reference Points:
Design in the Netherlands since 1945

William Deere

The German occupation of the Netherlands during World War II wreaked havoc on all aspects of Dutch life. The war presented leftist Dutch designers with two alternatives: to escape, or join the underground resistance. Tragically, graphic design lost several leading figures during the occupation, including H.N. Werkman, shot by the Germans in 1945, and Jean François van Royen, who died in a German camp in 1942. Some designers, such as Gerard Kiljan, Paul Schuitema, and Piet Zwart, fled to London, while others, such as Willem Sandberg, Otto Treumann, and Harry Sierman, stayed in the country and became part of the underground movement, creating illegal printed materials. Those designers who stayed, shaped by their wartime experience, brought a new sensibility to Dutch design, and later became the "new generation" of postwar Dutch designers.

Before the war Jean François van Royen was Secretary-General of the PTT (the Dutch postal and telecommunications agency). Van Royen's design commissions and dogmatic rejection of all that was ugly led to the establishment of the Department of Esthetics and Design (DEV), whose job was to commission art, architecture, products, and graphics that reflected the institutional excellence of the PTT. The precedent that Van Royen established endures today in the Kunst and Vormgeving Organization (Art and Design Office), formerly the DEV, which was renamed when the PTT was privatized in 1989. Although the original vision has changed somewhat with each DEV director's reign, the union of vanguard aesthetics with functional design for the PTT has continued.

During the 1950s, although the Netherlands and particularly Amsterdam was heading toward prosperity, graphic design witnessed little experimentation. Earlier innovators such as Schuitema and Zwart focused on teaching; the formal prinicples behind their exuberantly technological work from the prewar years was rejected by the high-visibility designers of the 40s and 50s, such as Dick Elffers, Willem Sandberg, and Otto Treumann, who moved towards a more painterly romanticism. Perhaps in response to the horrors of war, these men sought a more neutral approach to design, one less challenging to the war-weary public. Sandberg, director of the Stedlijk Museum (City Museum) for seventeen years, spoke of his disdain for sharp edges, preferring instead the softer aesthetic of torn paper—during the late 40s, even the PTT's stamp designs returned to traditional portraiture.

Typographic design by H.N. Werkman, 1924, from The Next Call 4, *issued on the occasion of Lenin's death.*

In January of 1963 design in the Netherlands witnessed the birth of a seminal and controversial design office: Total Design, founded by Wim Crouwel, Friso Kramer, Dick Schwarz, Paul Schwarz, and Benno Wissing. The Total Design concept was new: that one office would provide unembellished, functional design in both two and three dimensions. The office earnestly employed grids and pragmatic systems to solve its clients' needs. Working in teams, TD was able to take on large projects for private clients, museums, and government institutions. Total Design championed the use of systematic corporate identities or "house styles," which at that time were becoming an international phenomenon. The world's thriving free-market economy and the Netherlands' shift from a low- to a high-income country made the 1960s an opportune period for large-scale design commissions. The size of TD, which at times counted forty-plus employees, also allowed the firm to handle extensive, complex projects.

Wim Crouwel was the chief ideologue behind Total Design. During the early 1950s Crouwel was exposed to the work of Swiss designers such as Max Bill, Karl Gerstner, Josef Müller-Brockman, and others. Later, Crouwel turned away from the Swiss methodology, considering it too decorative; through TD, he produced his own interpretation of modernism, as revealed in his New Alphabet of 1967, a rectilinear typeface reduced to a minimal pattern of information, suggesting possibilities for the union of typography and the still infant realm of computer technology.

*Amsterdam Alphabet, created by Total Design
for an exhibition of work by Claes Oldenberg at
the Stedelijk Museum, 1970. This soft but systematic
alphabet shows the humorous side of rational
modernism.*

FEBRUARI

During this time of growth and prosperity for Total Design, the Graphische Vormgevers Nederland (the GVN, now known as beroepsvereniging Nederlandse Ontwerpers, or bNO) formed out of a merger of older artists' guild organizations. The professionalization of design provoked discussions about the proper approach to visual communication. Two opposing protagonists in many of these discussions were Crouwel and Jan van Toorn. Whereas Crouwel was committed to the pure transmittal of the client's message, Van Toorn believed that design should be augmented by an infusion of the designer's viewpoint. Van Toorn's skepticism about the ideal of value-free communication is influenced by the Marxist critique of the culture industry; he has used his design and teaching to explore the relationship between visual form and political power.

In addition to Total Design, other major design offices were formed in the 60s and 70s, including Tel Design, BRS, and Vorm Vijf. During this time, almost every graphic designer in the country came into contact with one or more of these offices, either as a student intern, free-lancer, or staff designer—even the fiercely unique designer Anthon Beeke was affliated with Total Design for a number of years in the late 70s.

Since its founding in 1969, BRS has been dedicated exclusively to graphic design, producing house styles, signage systems, annual reports, brochures, and magazines, often based on extensive research. After two decades of growth, BRS is now the largest graphic design office in the Netherlands.

Tel Design began as an industrial design office in the early 60s, but with the addition of Gert Dumbar in 1967 embraced graphic design also. It was during Dumbar's tenure that Tel landed such prestigious accounts as the Dutch Railways and the PTT house-style manual, the latter produced in conjunction with Total Design.

In 1977 Gert Dumbar left Tel to found Studio Dumbar in The Hague, taking with him major projects for the Dutch Railways and the PTT. Some of the studio's aesthetic momentum came from a reactionary rejection of Swiss rationalism and Crouwel's functional methodology

in favor of an emotional, expressive, and often humorous approach to design. This philosophy is seen, for example, in posters employing paper maché constructions and staged photography—reminiscent of Piet Zwart's work from the 30s—to wryly illustrate their subject matter. Staged photography, usually shot by Lex van Pieterson, has become one of the studio's hallmarks. The Dumbar style is also characterized by eccentric shapes, air brush gradations, *dingetjes* (little things), inventively fastidious typography, and general embellishment.

By the early 80s the office had become a magnet for *stagiaires* (student interns) from around the world, who poured into Studio Dumbar as they had into Total Design and Tel Design in the 70s; many returned after graduation for long-term positions. Dumbar has a symbiotic relationship with his staff: although he feeds off the talent cultivated in Dutch art schools, his designers benefit in turn from Dumbar's ability to charm clients into endorsing their ambitious, sometimes extravagant design solutions. Many gifted individuals have passed through Dumbar's doors, including Petr van Blokland, Ko Sliggers, Ric Comello, Henk Hoebé, Vincent van Baar, Ton van Bragt, Armand Mevis, Linda van Deursen, and Ton Homburg. These designers have since formed their own studios.

By restricting the size of his studio to ten or twelve designers, Dumbar has been able to undertake large projects while resisting pressure to accept banal commissions out of financial neessity. The studio has succeeded in bringing avant-garde aesthetics both to small cultural projects and to large commissions for government agencies and major corporations such as Apple, Philips, Wang, Shell, Aegon, and Centraal Beheer—substantial clients through which Dumbar has increased the public's awareness of design. Gert Dumbar has had an international impact through his contact with Cranbrook Academy of Art and London's Royal College of Art, lectures throughout the US, reproductions in countless magazines and books, and his studio's influence on student interns from around the world.

Theater poster advertising events at Studio Scarabee, a predecessor of Zeebelt Theater. Designed by Studio Dumbar. Photography by Lex van Pieterson.

Logo for the PTT, Holland's postal and telecommunications company, designed by Studio Dumbar.

Logo for NOB (Dutch Broadcasting Production Facilities), designed by Studio Dumbar, c.1988.

Logo for Aegon, a large insurance company, designed by Studio Dumbar.

Another important office is Hard Werken ("Working Hard"), founded in Rotterdam in 1980 by Gerard Hadders, Rick Vermuelen, Tom van den Haspel, Helen Howard, and Henk Elenga (who has since established Hard Werken LA Desk, in Los Angeles). Initially, Hard Werken was structured as a collective rather than an incorporated office; its members worked on their own projects and occasionally collaborated on larger ones. The structure became more business-like as the office grew.

An eclectic group more interested in the contemporary art scene than the regimentation of the International Style, Hard Werken is multidisciplinary, but in a more personal, idiosyncratic way than Total Design or Tel. Although some members of Hard Werken have worked three-dimensionally—notably Van Den Haspel and Elenga, whose lighting and furniture blurs the boundary between design and sculpture—the group never intended to be a full-service office in the mold of Total Design, and in fact is radically opposed to the rational philosophy governing TD. Although Hard Werken shares the maverick attitude of Studio Dumbar, its work has generally been less refined and in a sense less commercial; Hard Werken is often crude and abrasive, using strange combinations of colors and peculiar typefaces—letters that are distorted, damaged, or deliberately ordinary.

As we pass into the 90s, many young Dutch designers are looking at the work of Hard Werken and particularly Studio Dumbar as the face of the 80s, and now want to develop their own visual languages. Some are shifting away from complexity, personal interpretations, and such devices as staged photography towards a renewed interest in minimal communication, while others are evolving the traditions of Studio Dumbar, Hard Werken, BRS, and Vorm Vijv. Some of the most innovative work is in type design, thanks to advances in software. The Netherlands has always been a country of individuals, determined to express their opinions through art or politics or both. This commitment to individuality is seen in the numerous one-person studios and small partnerships that have formed; each is producing work that reflects its members' own views of the culture. It is these individuals—rather than large advertising design offices—who will resist the pressure exerted by Europe's changing economic structure and proceed to define Dutch graphic design's new idiom.

Logo for the publication Kunst uit Rotterdam, *designed by Hard Werken, 1984. The differences between Hard Werken and Studio Dumbar reflect their geographic locations: the royal town of The Hague is stately and genteel, while Rotterdam is a tough industrial city.*

Symbol designed by Berry van Gerwen for a moving announcement, c.1990.

Drawings for non-lining figures, for Scala, designed by Martin Majoor, 1988-1990. Distributed by FontShop.

NON-LINING FIGURES:
ON RECENT DUTCH TYPE DESIGN

Robin Kinross

Typeface design: "the fastest growing profession" in the Nether-lands.[1] There is an obvious technical explanation for the recent explosion of activity in designing typefaces: the availability the Apple Macintosh and programs such as Fontographer and Ikarus M. But the more intriguing question is this: Why such a concentration of type design in the Netherlands?

For the last 400 years the Low Countries have been a center for the design of letterforms. On the circuit of European typography, punches and punchcutters moved freely between the nodal cities: Paris, Antwerp, Amsterdam, Frankfurt, Leipzig, Basel... In the era of hot-metal and photocomposition (roughly 1900 through 1985), this international exchange continued, but change now occurred more slowly, dominated as it was by a few large companies. Now, with digital type and the microcomputer, things have become more open. Letters and their designers have become itinerant once again. Characters formed on a screen in an attic in The Hague, can join— later that evening—an electronic circuit whose nodal points include Berlin, London, New York, San Francisco...

THE DUTCH TRADITION
In this century, the pivotal figure in Dutch type design remains Jan van Krimpen (1892-1958). His work, especially the typefaces designed for his long-term employer, the typefounders and printers Joh. Enschedé en Zonen, summarizes the "classical" or "traditional" strand of Dutch typography. Both in his letterforms and in his design with text and image, one sees an immaculately controlled, austere yet pow-erful sensibility at work: a feeling that recalls ice cold *genever* (the Dutch gin). There is a cluster of designers whose individual contri-butions have been made in the wake of Van Krimpen: Dick Dooijes (1909), Sem Hartz (1912), Chris Brand (1921), and Bram de Does (1934).[2] Thus De Does's Trinité typeface, designed at Enschedé for photocomposition in 1979 and released in 1982, is, in its calligraphic delicacy, clearly in the Van Krimpen spirit.

Developing alongside classical Dutch typography was the mod-ernist avant-garde (the holy trinity of Piet Zwart, Paul Schuitema, and Gerard Kiljan), a group which barely engaged in letterform design, choosing instead to use available typefaces, preferably anonymously designed sans serif letters. Of course, this polarity of traditional/ modern was not absolute, even in the heydays of each strand; after 1945 it breaks down further, in pragmatic work (book design, especi-ally) without strict stylistic allegiances.

C. 48 NO. 4524 6 KG
ALLEEN KAPITALEN. CIJ

HET

C. 36 NO. 4523 8.50 K

Het be

C. 28 NO. 4522 7.50 K

He may

C. 24 NO. 4521 8 KG

Hier ist au

Lutetia, designed by Jan van Krimpen, 1925, Joh. Enschedé en Zonen, Haarlem.

In former da
shape a new

In former da
shape a new

In former da
shape a new

Trinité 1, 2, and 3, designed by Bram de Does, 1979. The digital version is scheduled for release by The Enschedé Font Foundry, 1992. Trinité is designed with three different lengths of ascenders and descenders.

1. This observation was made by Marjan Unger in an essay by herself and her hus-band Gerard Unger, "Dutch Landscape with Letters," *Gravisie* 14 (Utrecht: Van Boekhoven-Bosch, 1989). The same issue includes an essay by Max Caflisch on Dutch type design. See also Carel Kuitenbrouwer, "Wandeling door Neelands Typo-grafisch Landschap," *Items* 34 (1990).
2. Their work, together with Gerard Unger's, is summarized in Mathieu Lommen, *Letterontwerpers* (Haarlem: Joh. Enschedé en Zonen, 1987).

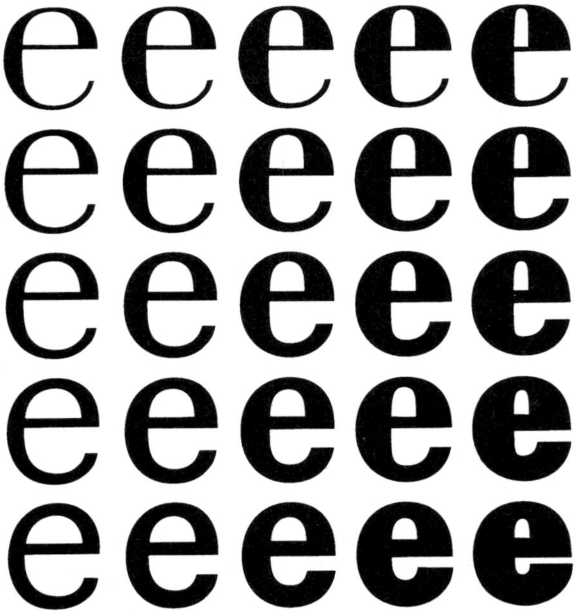

Gerrit Noordzij sees
all letters as formed by
translation,
as if produced by
a broad-nibbed pen,
or expansion, as
if produced by a pen
with a flexible nib.
His diagram shows
variations of contrast
in translation and
expansion.

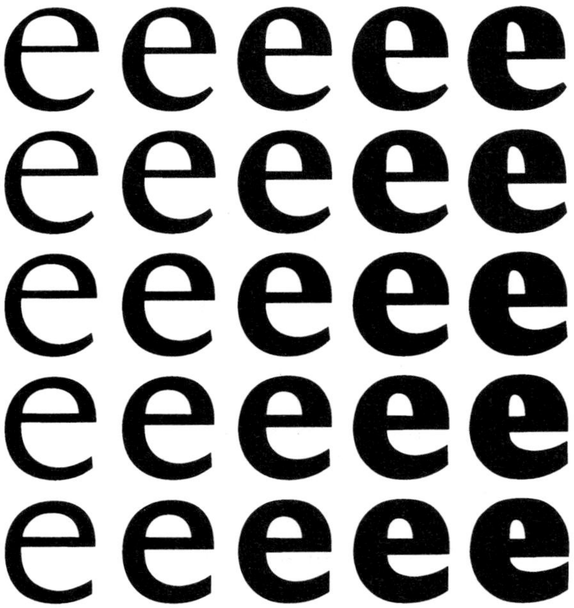

ABCDEFGH
IJKL MNO
STU
XYZ&
hijklm
tuvw
xyz
ghijkl
qrstu
xyz
67890

A Theory of Letters

Another central figure among the post-Van Krimpen designers is Gerrit Noordzij (1931), influential as a teacher as well as a graphic designer and typographer. In this latter role, over a long period at the Koninklijke Academie van Beeldende Kunsten (KABK) at The Hague, Noordzij has been a central presence in the phenomenon of the young type designers. He is someone with strong and coherent ideas allied to remarkable practical skills.

Noordzij founds his theories in the act of writing with a pen: either broad-nibbed or expanding.[3] This scheme provides a set of terms for understanding and describing all letters. His analysis of writing extends to a description of how component strokes are made, with a degree of detail that may be unmatched in the long history of letterform theory. Though Noordzij recognizes the differences between written forms and typefaces, he still places the practice of writing at the root of all work in letterform design, resulting in a powerful, pedagogically effective dogma. As Gerrit Noordzij's students develop beyond the obvious paths that his theories describe, they do so knowingly and from a strong base.

Critical Experiments

This element of critical and articulate consciousness about letters differentiates the emerging Dutch designers from their contemporaries in other countries. Too often, experiments by the latter have been exercises in pattern-making, with intellectual content reduced to the tired issue of "legibility." By contrast, take the now celebrated "Beowolf" experiment of two Hague graduates, Just van Rossum (1966) and Erik van Blokland (1967)—the two are sometimes known as "LetTerRor."[4] Van Rossum and Van Blokland have computer programming as well as drawing skills, and they used this knowledge to create Beowolf, a randomized font whose rough edges change slightly with each iteration. While Beowolf may be a Dada provocation, in the familiar Dutch manner, it also addresses a serious issue: it questions the over-immaculate smoothness and sharpness that has become an attainable ideal in printing, especially with perfect-bodied Californian PostScript fonts.

Beowolf is one of a series of experiments now pouring from the Hague LetTerRorists: handwriting type, ball-point pen type, a battered typewriter font, type that deteriorates over time... The randomizing influence can also be seen in Newberlin, from another Hague designer, Peter Verheul (1965). A severe display face—it is constructed

3. Noordzij's theory of writing is presented in his book *De Streek: Theorie van het Schrift* (Leersum: Uitgeverij ICS Nederland, 1991). An earlier version appeared in English as *The Stroke of the Pen* (The Hague: KABK, 1982). These theories have also been aired—in Noordzij's idiosyncratic English—in his bulletin *Letterletter*, published since 1984 by ATyPI from Münchenstein, Switzerland.
4. For a succinct exposition, see Erik van Blokland and Just van Rossum, "Is Best Really Better?" *Emigre* 18 (1991).

Remer, designed by Gerrit Noordzij.

Beowolf, randomized font designed by Erik van Blokland and Just van Rossum, 1990. The characters are different with each iteration, from Beowolf 21, which changes only slightly, to Beowolf 23, "a hectic face [that] beautifully represents the hurry and stress of modern life." Distributed by FontShop.

BCDEFGHIJKL
bcdefghijkl
EÑÖÜá

ABCDEF
WXYZab
yz ABCDE
O I 2 3 4 5 6

*Trixie Plain and
Justlefthand Regular,
designed by
Erik van Blokland and
Just van Rossum.*

leize regisnertra – fösche rubbosa
klabottchen hedest brepsch grasiel
*meiglich pfäßlich nud rabel. Öf
klabottchen hedest brepsch, grasiel*
foick, redo trasen-nonkufiration
nonkufiration.

erd Heibzig, na?
d imeschgrotz,
lpenheim, rieh!
d Juschnil Teick
erhaft.

*Newberlin, designed
by Peter Verheul.*

simply by joining outline points with straight lines—Newberlin is softened in alternative versions by a roughening of the edges. The work was done quickly, in spare time, and the typeface was soon released commercially by the FontShop network. Meanwhile, Verheul has been working on more complex projects, yet to appear, which demand all the skills and knowledge of traditional letterforms that he—like the other young Dutch designers—definitely has.

These skills are evident in a typeface designed by Petr van Blokland (1956), an information designer, part-time teacher at the KABK, and brother of Erik van Blokland. Proforma, designed for the Danish company Purup Electronics and still (at the time of this writing) being developed after several years of work. As a typeface for forms design, Proforma needs to include every kind of symbol, diacritical mark, and ligature: an extreme instance of the possibility now open to the digital type designer of "cutting" the final forms of all the characters. This solid capacity for carrying complex information is allied to a formally sophisticated letterform. Petr van Blokland has considerable computer programming expertise as well as traditional design abilities, a combination that has allowed him to work critically and reflectively (he was behind the adaptation of the Ikarus program for the Macintosh).

To round off this sketch of Hague type designers, one might refer to the work of Peter Matthias Noordzij (1961), the son of Gerrit Noordzij, and another designer whose work has begun to consolidate this synthesis of enlightened and traditional approaches. A graduate of the KABK, he now teaches there part-time, and has one major typeface to his name: PMN Caecilia for Linotype-Hell. This might be classified as a "slab-serif" or "Egyptian," but, especially in its italic, it has none of the lumpishness associated with this category. Peter Matthias Noordzij is now in charge of the recently established Enschedé Font Foundry. The Trinité family by De Does has been digitized, and Enschedé's program will take in typefaces designed by Gerrit Noordzij and Jan van Krimpen. The wheel seems to have turned full-circle.

Hambur

Hambur

HAMBUR

Hamburgefontiv

Hamburgefontiv

*Proforma, designed by
Petr van Blokland,
for Purup Electronics.*

functies van de
e terug bij het
cherp beeld
stoffen; een *dia-*
r zorgt dat de
niet overbelast
lijkheid om
instelling van de lens aan te
aan de afstand waarop het voor
zich bevindt, hetzij door de
van de lens tot de film te
(camera), hetzij door de *krom*

*PMN Caecilia, designed
by Peter Matthias Noordzij
for Linotype.*

This fusion of opposite delineate opposite poi or vice versa, and inste seems to r become al familiar al new unex

abcdefghijklmnopc
ABCDEFGHIJKLMN

abcdefg
ABCDE

Swift, designed by
Gerard Unger.

The Hague/Noordzij axis is not the only one that animates contemporary Dutch type design. Gerard Unger (1942) stands between generations, and in his early career worked through the worst years of typesetting—between the end of metal and the advent of digital.[5] His typefaces from that era are now being released in PostScript versions, and we are beginning to see them in action. Unger's Swift stands out as one of the most versatile and yet distinctive contributions of recent years. Designed as a newspaper face, it combines robustness—necessary for that function—with aesthetic refinement.

A fruitful source for young designers has been the school at Arnhem, where a series of distinguished book typographers have taught, including Jan Vermeulen, Alexander Verberne, and Karel Martens. In turn, some all-round typographers have graduated, who have included typeface design in their activities. Evert Bloemsma (1958) designed a typeface named Balance, that never was released commercially but could be seen in the headlines of the architectural magazine *Forum* between 1984 and 1987.

Martin Majoor (1960) is an Arnhem graduate. His typeface Scala (in which this publication is typeset), was designed originally for the Muziekcentrum Vredenburg at Utrecht; it has been released by the FontShop network and is beginning to be used widely. Scala sums up many characteristics of recent Dutch type design. It is an "old style" face, perhaps, but it follows no established model—it invokes memories of W. A. Dwiggins and Eric Gill. Scala has a definite, sharp character of its own, which escapes the Van Krimpen mold. As usual with the Dutch, the italic has a strong, insistent rhythm, perhaps to an extreme. Much love and attention has gone into the "special sorts"—there is even an x-height ampersand—and the figures are, of course, non-lining.[6]

Another Arnhem graduate, Fred Smeijers (1961) spent some years at Océ, the Dutch photocopier and laser-printer manufacturer, helping to introduce good standards to the firm's typeface output; he has since become a partner in the design studio Quadraat. He describes his typeface Amano as "the result of my discontent with Times and Plantin—Times being too stiff and too glittering, Plantin being a bit too heavy and a little bit too sturdy as well." Amano is scheduled for release in 1992 by Quadraat. Smeijers now teaches part-time at Arnhem, as does Majoor, who has also taken over Chris Brand's type design course at Breda. The tradition will continue.

Balance, designed by
Evert Bloemsma.

Amano, designed
by Fred Smeijers.
Scheduled for release
in 1992 by Quadraat.

DINSDAG 26 NOVEMBER - KONINK
DONDERDAG 28 NOVEMBER -
ZATERDAG 30 NOVEMBER - KONINI

O P E R
(IN SAMENWERKING MET H

S Y M I
O R k

KONINKLIJK
CONSERVATORIUM

INFORMATIE & KAARTVERKOOP:
[DEN HAAG] 070 - 381 42 51 / [UTRECHT] 030 - 310 241

5. For a brief survey of Unger's typefaces, see my own essay, "Technology, Aesthetics, and Type," *Eye* 3 (1991).

6. Lining figures are available if you want to look for them. An index of the passions that these small signs arouse: when Martin Majoor discussed Gerard Unger's article on Dutch type design (see note 1), the debate focused on the non-use of small capitals and non-lining figures in that publication (set in two typefaces by Unger). See *Compres* (March 20, 1990). Unger replied in the issue of May 1, 1990.

QUALIFICATIONS

These type designers exemplify the Dutch situation: a highly developed culture within a small geographical span. The skills, the critical thought, the tightly woven professional and educational networks: the Dutch culture of art and artisanship can become overwhelming. At that point the Dutch spin off into their deadpan Dada humor, as an escape from intensity. For the full sense of this, of course, you need to know their language. And maybe avant-garde Dutch graphics have slipped so easily into international design culture just because most outsiders don't know the language. It is more palatable that way: one pulls in the strange fish, ignorant of the disconcerting things he says to you. But, at its best, and when seen fully, Dutch work combines experiment with criticism, dissidence with respect for the norms. The up-and-down liveliness of non-lining figures shows in this in a microcosm.

Thanks to Fransje Berserik and Koosje Sierman for advice.

Drawings for the letter z, for Scala, designed by Martin Majoor, 1988-1990. Distributed by FontShop.

Backside of letter paper designed by Caroline Zeevat, Hard Werken, for the Centraal Museum, 1990. The paper was printed in brilliant orange, so that the ink shows through onto the other side.

THE END OF HOUSE STYLE?
A GRAPHIC DESIGN PROJECT AT
THE CENTRAAL MUSEUM, UTRECHT

Daan de Kuyper

At the Centraal Museum, situated in the Dutch city of Utrecht, a remarkable graphic design project was started in January 1990 which challenged common assumptions about institutional identity, or "house style." The creator of the project was Sjarel Ex, who had recently been installed as the director of the museum. His proposition was startling and unorthodox: instead of a uniform house style, his ambition was to invite several designers to generate a gamut of diverse styles.

The effect of heterogeneity which Ex sought after departed from commonly accepted notions in the museum world (and elsewhere) regarding the utilitarian function of graphic design. As in other countries, the Dutch graphic designer is generally expected to develop a corporate identity program which will provide the client with a stable public image. In the Netherlands in the 1960s and 70s, the Total Design group had established the concept of corporate identity as an axiom of contemporary design practice.[1] The overpowering presence of Total Design in Holland often had resulted in uninspired work, which formulaically applied a set of rules in order to achieve formal clarity and immediate legibility. To guard the purity of typography as a neutral medium of communication was considered of paramount importance. [2]

PRELUDE

Shortly after Ex's inauguration as director of the Centraal Museum in 1988, he formed the idea of subverting the standard of "good" design set by Total Design in the preceding decades, whose position had become eroded in the contemporary landscape of Dutch graphic design. The existing house style of the Centraal Museum was, moreover, a drab, stereotypical version of functionalismn, and had not even been consistently implemented. These factors were provocation enough for Ex to impress his own "mark" on the museum's design policy. In the month of June 1989 Sjarel Ex approached me with his idea for setting up a new graphic design program in the museum, and asked me to manage its implementation. He proposed to discontinue the use of a consistent house style in the Centraal Museum, and to replace it with a range of different "styles."

Ex considered such a multitude of appearances, which he called the "no-total-design-style," especially appropriate for his museum with its pluriform collection.

1. Wim Crouwel (1928) founded Total Design in 1963 and remained co-director till 1980. Currently, Crouwel is director of the Museum Boymans-Van Beuningen in Rotterdam.
2. Hugues Boekraad, "Stijl en Signaturen," *Zeezucht* 2 (May 1989): 12.

Ex phrased his intentions as follows: "In this museum, after all, nobody swears by Univers or Helvetica, and should it not be possible that a temporary notice in one of the galleries is designed by Anthon Beeke, without his taking care of everything else as well?" Ex concluded that only a gamut of styles is capable of "acknowledging the Hydra character of the museum."[3] The Centraal Museum dates back as a municipal art foundation, and its holdings contain a range of heterogeneous materials: there is a department for antique and modern applied arts, several period rooms, a costume collection, a department for civic history, an important group of Dutch seventeenth-century paintings, and a separate wing for the exhibition of modern and contemporary art.

In practical terms Ex's proposal meant that many individual designers would be engaged in developing the museum's printed matter, an idea which was viewed with Argus eyes by the museum staff, who wondered if the plan could ever function efficiently and economically. The project would have had little chance of success without the Netherlands' climate of extensive government support for the arts, including a national endowment for design, created to stimulate the development of innovative projects like ours.

FINANCIAL SUPPORT

The Utrecht design project was a prime candidate for subsidy from the Department of Design in the Dutch Ministry of Culture. The department had ruled that in order to obtain funding from the national endowment for "commissions in the area of design," the policy of the applying institution must lead to a stimulation of new developments in Dutch design. It was easy to argue that our project complied with the stipulations drawn up by the grant agency. After all, the notion of the museum as a kind of laboratory in which one could freely experiment would certainly stimulate the formation of new ideas concerning graphic design in the Netherlands.

For the anticipated number of commissions, I selected around fifty graphic designers. Beforehand, we had decided they should come from divergent backgrounds and have differing degrees of professional experience; my list included young graphic designers who were just starting out on their careers, as well as those who were slightly older and had been important in breaking with the mold of Total Design, such as Rick Vermeulen and Gerard Hadders of Hard Werken in Rotterdam, members of Studio Dumbar in The Hague, and Anthon Beeke from Amsterdam.[4] The invitation of designers of

3. Sjarel Ex, in application for government grant.
4. Studio Dumbar was founded in the late 70s; Hard Werken ("Working Hard") was founded in 1980. The members of Hard Werken and the designers who work for Gert Dumbar (1940) became well-known for their playful approach to typography and their use of "staged photography." The design of Anthon Beeke (1940), who has usually worked on his own, has always been experimental, and does not fit easily into general categories of style or method.

an older generation together with the recent academy graduates promised to yield a provocative mixture. We were curious to see if any new patterns of paternalism had evolved.

The ultimate goal of the Utrecht project was to establish a broad survey of the state of design in the Netherlands. We decided to make this unique collection of products accessible to the public by means of a subscription system, which would help increase both moral and financial support for our project. For a relatively low cost (around $125), the subscriber would receive all the museum's printed matter for the duration of the project. A condition of the grant was that 70% had to be allocated to designers' fees, so the subscription system would also help to accommodate the expected high production costs.

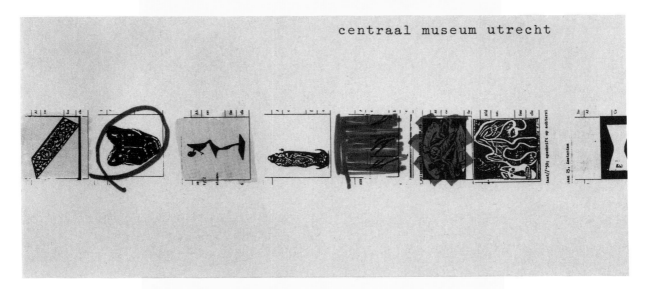

THE PROJECT PROCEEDS

The first commission went to Mart Warmerdam, whose task was to design a new information pamphlet for the museum.[5] He did not seek the solution in a glossy format, but gave it a more casual appearance. After certain indications from our side, he decided to emphasize the informal aspects of his first draft. He discarded the conventional vertical format of the old brochure and made the cover from brown paper—almost like wrapping paper. Along the top margin "Centraal Museum" was printed in an unpretentious typewriter font.

5. Mart Warmerdam lives and works in Amsterdam. He graduated from the Rietveld Academy in the mid-80s and has received commissions from, for instance, Museum Boymans-van Beuningen, where Wim Crouwel is the current director.

Ex encouraged Warmerdam to introduce references to the disparate holdings of the museum. On the cover Warmerdam put reproductions of art works which can be found clipped onto the inventory cards of the museum. He increased the improvised look of the whole by marking the photographs with bright felt tip pens.

Warmerdam's pamphlet confounds ordinary expectations of how a museum addresses its public. Design is not perceived here as the presentation of factual information in a neutral manner, but the medium itself is used to tell a "story" about the museum. Warmerdam's approach stands in sharp contrast to a notion of "objective" standards in graphic design, which would deny the use of narrative or expressive devices. Significantly, the general personnel of the museum were surprised by the "sloppiness" of the brochure; apparently, it disturbed their deeply ingrained notions about museum decorum.

Meanwhile, I had given to five different designers the assignment of developing new letter paper. The first to be invited was Kees de Bruijn, of the studio Het Verre Oosten in Arnhem.[6] His initial drafts were cautious, and strongly determined by the concept of a house style. After encouragement from our side, he stepped away from the idea that the letter

6. The name of the design bureau, Het Verre Oosten ("The Far East"), refers to its location in Arnhem, near the eastern border of the Netherlands. Most designers practice in the Randstad-area (the part of Holland enclosed by Amsterdam, The Hague, Rotterdam, and Utrecht). "Het Verre Oosten" is run by Kees de Bruijn and Richard Derks, who are both graduates of the academy in Arnhem, which is closer in its teaching to functionalism than the Rietveld Academy of Amsterdam.

paper must have an official, functional look. He then chose brown wrapping paper as the material; however, he still remained within relatively "safe" margins by limiting his personal contribution to inventing a logo for the museum. The logo, which consisted of a propeller inscribed with the words "Centraal Museum," was meant to visualize the dynamism with which Ex wished to infuse the museum, in contrast to its former image as a low-key institution of mostly provincial stature. The logotype's most remarkable feature is the hole in its central axis, which literalizes the theme of energetic movement.

The examples of Warmerdam and De Bruijn show that it was not self-evident how a particular commission should be viewed within the larger framework of the Utrecht project. For instance, the design of Kees de Bruijn leans heavily on the rather conventional idea of a logotype, which could be (too) easily transferred onto an envelope or other item. The difficulty probably was caused by the absence of any specific guidelines: the designers did not know what was expected of them. It was clearly disconcerting to be in a position of greater freedom, where experimentation was possible and the pressure existed to invent in a way that is expected of fine artists.

Among the first five designs for letter paper, there is an instance in which the designer eagerly accepted the margin of freedom the project was meant to open up. Berry van Gerwen's design process started with a work by the Dutch sixteenth-century painter Hendrick ter Brugghen, a key-work in the museum's collection.[7] Van Gerwen admired the image of *The Merry Drinker* on a personal level; the painting's vertical format also made it suitable for his purposes. The reproduction of the painting is printed on the backside of the letter paper, so that it shines through on the front side, and forms a frame within which the text of the letter can be written. *The Merry Drinker* was also given two captions, deriving from separate museum catalogues, which notify the reader of such facts as date of creation, inventory-number, and size. The letter resembles a page torn out of one of the museum's catalogues—there is even a page number on each side of the sheet. To further emphasize his concept, Van Gerwen printed two letterheads on one sheet, so that the user had to tear them loose as if they were ripped out of a book.

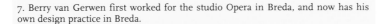

7. Berry van Gerwen first worked for the studio Opera in Breda, and now has his own design practice in Breda.

Van Gerwen printed the name of the museum in a brown half-circle, and shifted it off the center of the page. The top sections of the letters have been cut off, but the whole remains legible. Similar to Kees de Bruijn in his design, Berry van Gerwen left the letter-head typography intact, offering a cue for the person who received the sheet in the mail that it was indeed a letter from the museum.

The montage-like, fragmentary design of Van Gerwen was more successful than that of De Bruijn in expressing the impermanent character of the Utrecht project.

A third letterhead was designed by Martijn Swart.[8] In his first draft he worked with a broad frame around the paper. In order to achieve the right effect, he had constructed an actual frame in his studio and photographed it. In the frame he had included various objects; it was a small step from there to think of making a frame with objects from the museum collection. Ex granted him permission to use a group of medieval silver pieces, which were to be exhibited soon. Swart set up the final photo-shot with the photographer Ernst Moritz. They used an enormous plaster model of a picture frame, and cast long, dark shadows across the image with bright spotlights. The letter was printed in full color.

The extravagant, unrestrained quality of Martijn Swart's letterhead evoked numerous enthusiastic responses. One might even call the design irreverent, because of the seemingly nonchalant display of the priceless silver collection. The illusionism of the letter design (the use of a model with an over-extended scale, shadows running over the paper, references to painting, etc.) would be abhorrent to a functionalist theorist like Total Design's Wim Crouwel, who wrote that the two-dimensional and the three-dimensional can be combined, but that the borderline must never be blurred: "Photography introduces on paper the third dimension, whereas typography is concerned with the surface. As a designer you have to combine those two divergent elements so that you achieve a stratification on the page. One must avoid the use of perspectival devices and the imitation of nature. The photograph already does that."[9] Swart had no fear of overstepping such boundaries in his pursuit of hybrid effects, which could be termed a functionalist nightmare. Most striking in this respect is the typographic element of the letterhead, which no longer represents a pure flat surface, but appears to hover in an indeterminate space, as a result of the created illusion.

The lavishness of Martijn Swart's paper is closely matched by a pamphlet which Armand Mevis and Linda van Deursen designed for the same silver exhibition.[10] Perhaps the most appealing aspect of this design was its use of silver foil-print on the cover. A small booklet about the exhibition is wrapped within the cover, which itself can be detached from the booklet and transformed into a poster by folding it out. In its fully opened form, we see the blackened face of a silver mine worker and the chemical symbol for silver, "Ag," while on the reverse side the layout of the exhibition is explained and supplemented by photographs. Mevis and Van Deursen also designed the invitation for the exhibition.

8. Martijn Swart graduated from the academy in The Hague in the mid-80s, and has established an independent practice in Amsterdam.
9. Wim Crouwel, "Op een afstand," in "Grafische vormgeving verhoudt zich tot de beeldende kunst," special issue of *Lecturis* 20 (June 1990): 26.
10. Armand Mevis and Linda van Deursen are two designers from Amsterdam who graduated with Mart Warmerdam from the Rietveld Academy. They have been collaborators since the beginning of their careers.

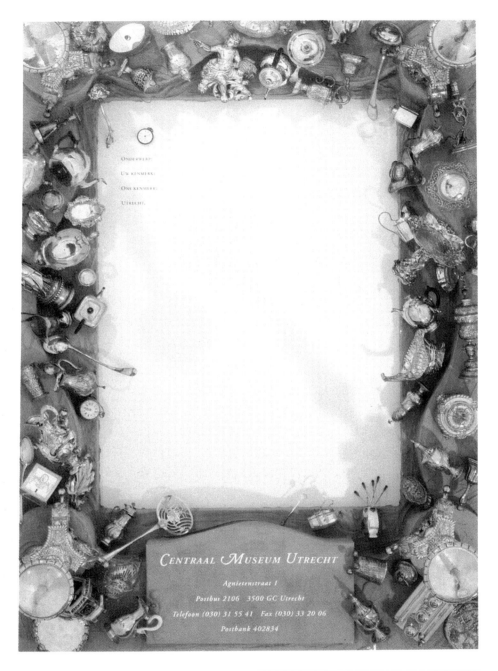

Letter paper designed by Martijn Swart
for the Centraal Museum, Utrecht, featuring
a staged photograph of priceless silver from
the museum's collection.

Pamphlet for an exhibition of silver, designed by Armand Mevis
and Linda van Deursen for the Centraal Museum, Utrecht.
The blackened face of the silver mine worker contrasts with the
glittering luxury of the objects on view in the exhibition.
The chemical symbol for silver, "Ag," is printed at the bottom.

The final example I will mention is the pair of envelopes designed by Jan-Paul de Vries.[11] De Vries has given each envelope an outlandish appearance by covering its pristine surface with a fragmented, partly crossed out and annotated text. In a reversal of inside and outside, the private realm of a letter is spilled out onto the surface. The envelope draws the viewer in, enticing her to spell out the half-obliterated text. For one envelope, De Vries used a letter written to Ex by a formerly faithful visitor to the museum, who had become angered by the director's "tampering" with the installation of the collections. The text on the other letter is extracted from the statement Ex wrote for the grant application. On one of the envelopes, a red cross has been drawn through the return addresss: this bold little mark concisely articulates the unwillingness of the museum to adopt a stable public image, unless it is precisely that of a 'lack' of identity.

Geachte ... van de comm ...,

Centraal Museum ...

... Posbus ... 3500 G ...

in N... Zo'n u... ... van ...

... actie ... G. R...

The Centraal Museum project requires a large amount of time, energy and money. Although it probably will be difficult to secure enough resources in the future to sustain the project, this does not invalidate the philosophy behind it. The project's aim to achieve a diverse and unpredictable effect has already been fulfilled. A misunderstanding would arise if the non-house style were judged in terms other than those in which it was originally conceived—the pluriform and changing nature of the project thus could be viewed as the "new identity" of the Centraal Museum. Ironically, the non-house style is then subsumed under the old idea of corporate identity—a notion against which the whole project was directed in the first place.

11. Jan-Paul de Vries worked for Samenwerkende Ontwerpers in Amsterdam. Earlier he was an intern at Hard Werken.

GRAPHIC DESIGN IN THE NETHERLANDS: A SELECTION OF RECENT WORK

On the following pages is a selection of work by emerging graphic designers from the Netherlands. Many of these figures were formerly associated with high-profile offices such as Studio Dumbar, Hard Werken, and Vorm Vijv; most have since established their own studios or partnerships, sometimes in their homes or apartments. The designers featured on the following pages—with the exceptions of Henrik Barends, Reynoud Homan, and Ton Homburg—graduated from Dutch art schools during the mid-1980s: their voices are setting the tone of graphic design in the 90s.

There is no single stylistic principle uniting these emerging designers: their common ground is the Dutch culture. Elements of the modernist avant-garde pervade much of the work, as revealed in the fascination with systematic structure, the techniques of mechanical production, and the photographic sign. The deliberately inventive, visually confrontational aspect of the work reflects a notion of design as an avant-garde practice—a model more prevalent in Europe than in North America, where graphic design is often viewed primarily as a marketing instrument. Also present in contemporary Dutch design are memories of the older arts of Netherlandish still-life painting, book-making, and engraving, with their proclivity for empirical observation and ornamental detail. The work is open to influences from contemporary mass culture as well: the Netherlands is a tiny country, but it is centrally positioned in the world economy. Most of the examples shown here were produced for cultural clients, including galleries, theaters, publishers, and arts councils. While innovative design is also commissioned by large corporations—such as the PTT, the country's most prominent design client—many independent designers are enjoying the opportunity to work within Holland's tremendously fertile cultural arena: an arena in which their own work is understood to play a serious artistic role.

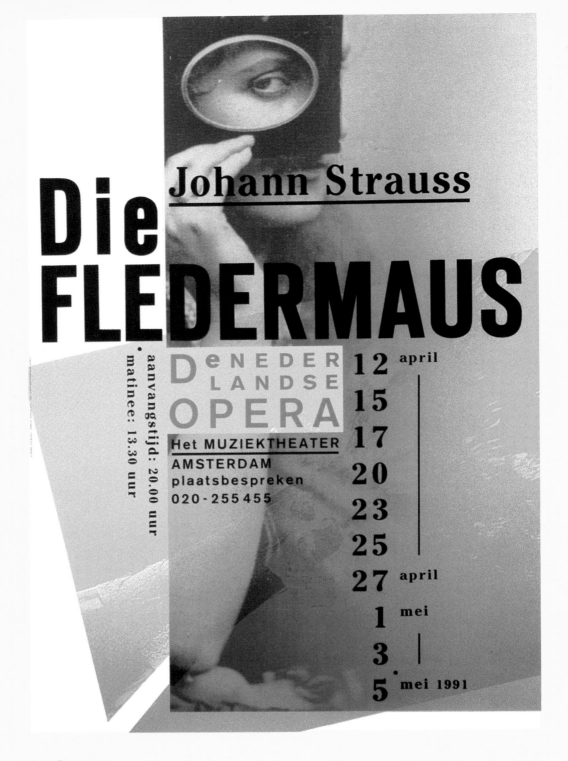

Johann Strauss

Die FLEDERMAUS

aanvangstijd: 20.00 uur
matinee: 13.30 uur

De NEDER
LANDSE
OPERA

Het MUZIEKTHEATER
AMSTERDAM
plaatsbespreken
020-255455

12 april
15
17
20
23
25
27 april
1 mei
3 .
5 mei 1991

LEX REITSMA

Since graduating from Amsterdam's Rietveld Academy in 1983, Lex Reitsma has worked as an independent designer, currently in Haarlem. One of his long-term clients has been the Netherlands Opera, for whom he produces posters and program books. In his posters, Reitsma focuses on the verbal message—time, place, title, etc.—as a major design element, rather than subordinating the text to an overwhelming image. Each of the program books for the Opera has its own typographic identity; the images are selected to poetically comment on the content or style of the opera, rather than documenting the actors and staging of a particular production.

Zeg eens: als straks een van ons
zal moeten sterven, hij of ik,
en aan jou zou de beslissing zijn,
wie zou je dan de dood in sturen,
wiens reddende engel zul je zijn?

Marija

Ach, genoeg, kwel me niet zo!
Leidt me niet in verzoeking.

Mazeppa

Geef antwoord!

Marija

Je bent bleek, je stem klinkt verbeten.
O, wees niet boos. Alles, alles
zal ik voor je doen, geloof me.
Maar je woorden maken me bang.
Zwijg nu.

Mazeppa

Onthoud je woorden goed, Marija,
onthoud wat je nu zegt.

(Vertaald door Aaldert van den Bogaard)

24

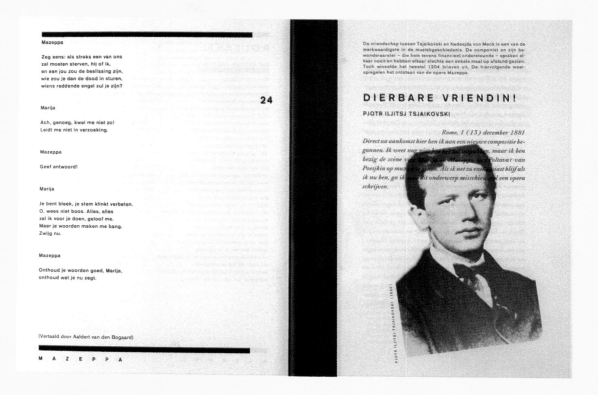

De vriendschap tussen Tsjaikovski en Nadesjda von Meck is een van de merkwaardigste in de muziekgeschiedenis. De componist en zijn bewonderaarster – die hem tevens financieel ondersteunde – spraken elkaar nooit en hebben elkaar slechts een enkele maal op afstand gezien. Toch wisselde het tweetal 1204 brieven uit. De hiervolgende weerspiegelen het ontstaan van de opera Mazeppa.

DIERBARE VRIENDIN!

PJOTR ILJITSJ TSJAIKOVSKI

Rome, 1 (13) december 1881

Direct na aankomst hier ben ik aan een nieuwe compositie begonnen. Ik weet nog niet ... *maar ik ben bezig de scène* ... *Mazeppa* ... *Poltava van Poesjkin op muziek* ... *Als ik net zo enthousiast blijf als ik nu ben, ga ik* ... *dit onderwerp misschien wel een opera schrijven.*

PJOTR ILJITSJ TSJAIKOVSKI (1860)

De goddelijke komedie.

Dante Alighieri.

Paradijs — Canto V.

'De grootste gave die de Schepper in zijn mildheid aan de mensen schonk, en die het meest in overeenstemming was met zijn goedheid en door hemzelf ook het hoogst werd geschat, was die van de vrije wil: daarmee zijn de redelijke schepselen, zowel allen te samen als ieder afzonderlijk, vroeger en nu altijd begiftigd geweest. En als ge van hieruit logisch verder redeneert, zal u snel duidelijk worden hoe hoog de waarde van een belofte is, gesteld dat die aan de voorwaarde voldoet dat wanneer de mens ja zegt, ook God ja zegt. Want het is zo dat men bij het aangaan van het verbond tussen God en mens dit kostbare geschenk van de vrije wil waarover ik het hier heb, opoffert. En daarmee stelt men een weloverwogen daad. En wat voor een vergoeding kan er dan voor het niet nakomen ervan worden gegeven? Als ge meent dat ge dat wat ge hebt weggegeven nog kunt gebruiken, dan is het net of ge een goed werk wilt doen met gestolen geld. Van het belangrijkste punt zijt ge nu op de hoogte.

[...]

Er zijn twee zaken die tot het wezen van deze offerdaad behoren: bij de ene gaat het om datgene wat men offert, de andere betreft de overeenkomst zelf. Deze laatste kan pas worden opgeheven wanneer ze is nagekomen. En het is over haar dat ik hierboven in zo duidelijke bewoordingen heb gesproken. [...]

GELOFTE
IDOMENEO.

GELOFTE
IDOMENEO.

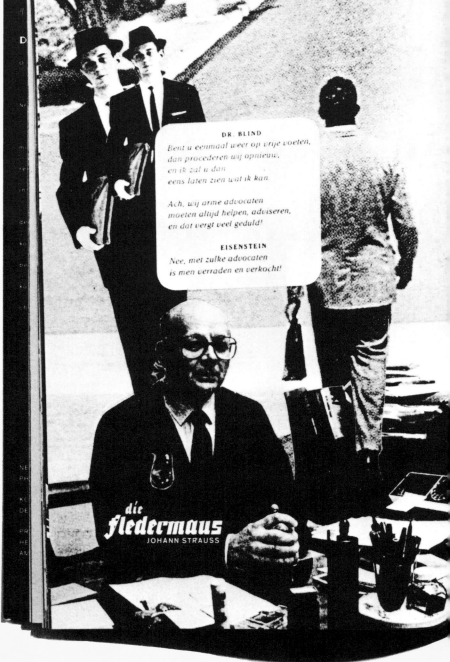

In the program created for the opera *Fledermaus*, Lex Reitsma sought to capture the stereotypical aspect of the characters with collages invoking an old film book. Reitsma explains that he and the printer (Mart. Spruijt) worked very hard to make the book look coarse and cheap.

Dr. Blind

Advokat

– – In het verloop van het aanvankelijk wegens schennis van de openbare eerbaarheid aangespannen proces ontstond tevens de verdenking dat in een ruimte grenzend aan de bar van het koffiehuis, de buitengewoon luxueus ingerichte "Turkse kamer", met grote regelmaat en met medeweten van de kastelein onzedelijke handelingen z o u d e n   z i j n   g e p l e e g d. In verband hiermee werd tegen Scheffel dan ook een aanklacht wegens gelegenheid geven krachtens § 515 W.v.S. ingediend. – –

– – M e t   b e t r e k k i n g   t o t   deze Turkse kamer had hij verklaard dat hij d i t   v e r t r e k   zelf naar orientaals voorbeeld met buitengewone luxe had ingericht, dat het vertrek een plafondverlichting bezat bestaande uit 4 8 0 g l o e i l a m p e n   en dat dit vertrek, dat voor voornaam gezels c h a p   was bestemd, ook en inzonderheid een achter een muurkast verborgen, naar de keldergang leidende, geheime uitgang had. Voorts heeft verdachte toegegeven dat in de Turkse kamer gezien de kostbare i n r i c h t i n g slechts sekt te drinken werd geserveerd, maar dat voor zover hem bekend in g en o e m d e   T u r k s e   k a m e r   nimmer ontuchtige handelingen zouden zijn gepleegd.

– – B i j   zijn schuldigverklaring aan schennis van de openbare eerbaarheid overwoog de rechter dat de heer Scheffel zich naar uit de bewijsvoering was gebleken jegens een werkneemster in de telefooncel en jegens een andere werkneemster in de vestiaire onzedelijk had gedragen op een wijze die in staat moest worden geacht aanstoot te geven. Het optreden van deze aanstoot behoefde, aldus de rechter, niet dadelijk op het gewraakte gedrag te zijn gevolgd; het volstond dat het onzedelijk gedrag van verdachte door derden waar te nemen en naderhand o n d e r w e r p v a n   d i s c u s s i e   was geweest.

– – B i j   zijn veroordeling wegens gelegenheid geven als bedoeld in § 515 W.v.S. overwoog de rechter allereerst m e t   b e t r e k k i n g   t o t   de Turkse kamer dat dit vertrek weliswaar, zoals verdachte stelde, als W e e n s e   b e z i e n sw a a r d i g h e i d   m a g   g e l d e n   en inderdaad naar orientaals voorbeeld was ingericht, maar dat bij het gerechtelijk onderzoek ter plaatse de eerste indruk v a n genoemd vertrek was geweest dat dit vertrek geenszins voor o ns c h u l d i g e,   s e r i e u z e,   beschaafde conversatie was bestemd maar daarentegen was bestemd om personen van beiderlei kunne in staat te stellen tot ongestoord samenzijn. Voorts was, aldus de overweging, uit de bewijsvoering gebleken dat in genoemde T u r k s e   k a m e r   ontuchtige handelingen als bedoeld in § 515 waren verricht, en dat deze ontuchtige incidenten t e v e n s   v a n   b u i t e n a f   d o o r   h e t v e n t i l a t i e l u i k   k o n d e n   w o r d e n   gadegeslagen. Dat verdachte, hoewel hij zulks loochende, kennis droeg van wat zich in d e   T u r k s e   k am e r   afspeelde, zou blijken uit het feit dat in T u r k s e   k a m e r   voorn o e m d   consumptie van sekt verplicht was, en voorts uit de m o r e e l - z e d el i j k e   d i s p o s i t i e   van de kastelein en de bestemming van d e   T u r k s e   k a m e r. – –

KARL KRAUS, WIE DIE ÖSTERREICHISCHE SITTLICHKEIT SPRICHT

(UIT: VOR DER WALPURGISNACHT)

Reitsma sees this page from a 1984 report for a government art commission as a watershed in his typographic approach. The book outraged people with its reckless—yet readable—pages. He explains, "The newspapers called it 'drunk typography.'"

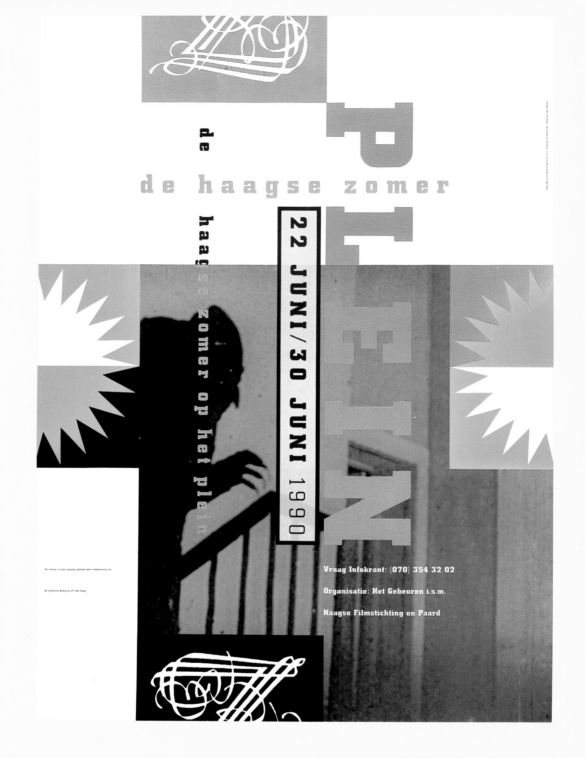

BEN FAYDHERBE *and* WOUT DE VRINGER
Now an independent partnership, Ben Faydherbe
and Wout de Vringer formerly worked with
the large-scale design studio Vorm Vijf.
Both are graduates of the Koninklijke Academy
in The Hague. Their posters incorporate vernacu-
lar materials drawn from the classical tradition
of Dutch printing and engraving as well as from
the contemporary mass media.

de *Haagse*

ZOMER

PLEIN

21 Pt/m 25 Njuni

1989

73 LF 36

ORGANISATIE **HET GEBEUREN** I.S.M. HAAGSE FILMSTICHTING, OOYEVAER DESK EN PAARD

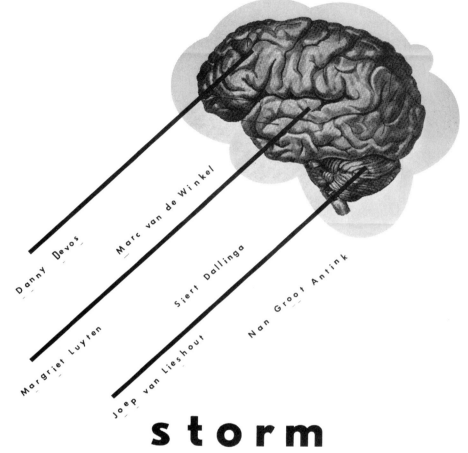

Brain-

Danny Devos

Marc van de Winkel

Siert Dallinga

Nan Groot Antink

Margriet Luyten

Joep van Lieshout

storm

1 september - 23 september

opening: zaterdag 1 september 16.00 uur

artis

openingstijden: do. t/m zo. 13.00 - 17.00 uur

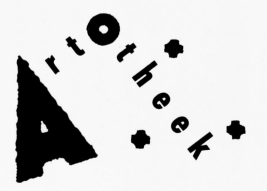

<small>BERRY VAN GERWEN</small>
Working with his partner Jan Bolle in Breda, Berry van Gerwen has managed to combine a typically Dutch attention to typographic detail with a flair for illustration and image-making which gives his work an unusual Pop edge. His invitation for the exhibition *Brainstorm* (ABOVE) literalizes the title of the show in a deliberately blunt, "artless" way. He explains, "I have my own handwriting, but I'm not really interested in style. I am trying to work as *directly* as possible" Artotheek (LEFT) is a government organization which leases works of art. Van Gerwen is a graduate of St. Joost Academy in Breda.

op vrijdag 23 september 1988   17.00 uur

OPENING

van

BRUTTO GUSTO

de bloemenwinkel van Geer Pouls

U bent van harte welkom

Brutto gusto

Oostkousdijk 12a (zijstraat Westzeedijk)

3024 CM Rotterdam-Delfshaven

010 42 59 441

ERIK ANDRIESSE

tekeningen

23 september tot 6 november

openingstijden

dinsdag t.m. vrijdag 11.00 tot 17.00 uur

zaterdag 10.00 tot 13.00 uur

Van Gerwen's series of invitations for Brutto Gusto in Rotterdam exemplifies the range and spirit of his work. Brutto Gusto (Italian for "bad taste") is a combined art gallery and flower shop. There is nothing sentimentally sweet, however, about either the gallery or Van Gerwen's invitations: the connotations they invoke range from the fascination with decay found in traditional Dutch still life painting (ABOVE) to a psuedo-corporate crispness (RIGHT).

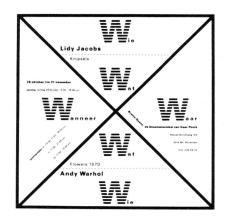

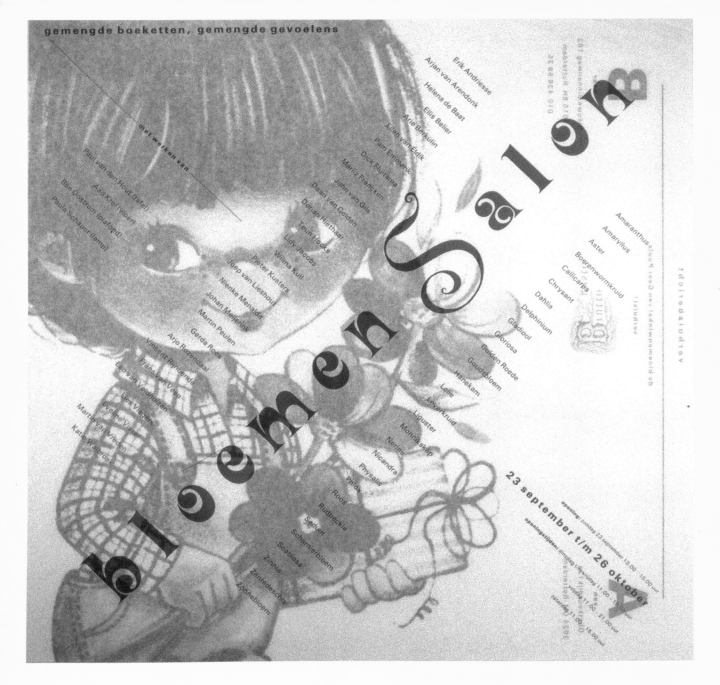

When Berry van Gerwen's flower invitations *do* invoke sentimentality, it's in a humorous spirit: the wide-eyed child of knick-knack culture (ABOVE) is combined with a 1960s-revival Art Nouveau alphabet. A similarly candied purple hue undercuts the avant-garde seriousness of the Brutto Gusto invitation at RIGHT.

verantwoordelijkheid

IN

BEELD

PETRA JANSSEN

The Amsterdam studio Boot ("boat") is
headed by Petra Janssen, who graduated
from the Koninklijke Academy in 1989.
The book cover ABOVE indicates her
bold, frank style, which departs from the
subtle layering commonly associated
with "Dutch design." Janssen's own
business card (LEFT) also exhibits her
characteristic directness.

Petra Janssen

BOOT
Grafische/Illustratieve/Mode
VORMGEVING
Werfpad 3C 5212 VJ
's-Hertogenbosch
Telefoon 073 - 143593

zondag 27 januari 1991 · 15.30 uur · fl. 7.50
TOM CORA
Cello Solo
HET APOLLOHUIS
TONGELRESESTRAAT 81 EINDHOVEN
5613 DB. HOLLAND
TELEFOON 040-440393

DAVID
TURN TABLES
SHEA
VRIJDAG 3 MEI 1991
HET APOLLOHUIS
TONGELRESESTRAAT 81 EINDHOVEN
5613 DB. HOLLAND
TELEFOON 040-440393
21.00 UUR FL 7,50

DUO

Arnold Dreyblatt   Paul Panhuysen

geloso

Duetten en solo's **op zelfgebouwde,** verbouwde en traditionele instrumenten, die verwijzen **naar rock en roll,** klassieke, etnische en **minimale muziek**

VRIJDAG 18 DECEMBER   **21.00 UUR**   ENTREE fl. 7,50

TON HOMBURG

The design studio Opera was founded by Ton Homburg in Breda in 1981. Homburg, who previously worked with Studio Dumbar, has since become one of Holland's most respected designers. Homburg's series of music posters for Het Apollohuis (1987-91) show his ability to create arresting graphics on a minimal budget. Each poster is printed in one color.

Linda van Deursen *and* Armand Mevis
Since graduating from the Rietveld Academy in 1986, Linda van Deursen and Armand Mevis have worked together. Whenever possible, they take an active role in shaping the concept and content of their projects, instead of delivering a straightforward "service" to their clients. Both are deeply involved in the art world, and view design as a critical and conceptual activity related to the fine arts. The exhibition catalogue *Hover Hover* (1991) is a collaboration with the artist Gerald van der Kaap. The book was conceived as an instructional "manual" for navigating through Van Der Kaap's exhibition, rather than as a conventional catalogue of works. The text includes a heavily footnoted and annotated interview with the artist. Van Deursen explains, "Armand and I want our work to 'up-to-date,' of this time. We want our designs to look 'actual'—that is, related to the everyday language of advertising and commercial publicity."

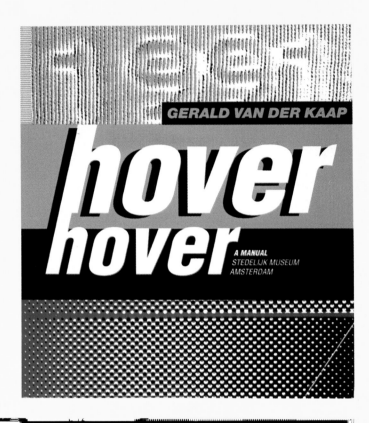

Although every effort was made to ensure the accuracy of thoughts appearing in this manual, it should be kept in mind that happiness can and does fluctuate in the course of time.

conTENTS

05	preface by W.A.L. Beeren
06	student dive tube web installation views
14	QA welcome to the hover house
17	style confidence: modern sleep myself
20	the works
25	the adulterated new
29	how to hover: don'ts & do's
32	free
37	brazilian adventure
52	thank you

inHOUD

	zaaloverzichten	
VA	30
interview door Dorine Mignot	
de werken	
niet wel	

reflex ; ?	! ; generate
consumer activism	so what
sky-dive; fall (g)	*hover hover (low-g/zero-g)*
DON'T	**DO**
weefgetouw	zweefgetouw
the 80's	**the 90's**
60's (zero)	(digital zero) 10's
i = information E.T.	$\sqrt{-1} = i$ *(as in happY)* E.V. (en ville)
true	**yes, negative**
deconstructing lies...............	constructing lies........ (using carnivalesque strategies)
mirrors	windows (0.1 portholes)
(...)	*the adulterated new*
everyday sign systems transformed into new meaning	new sign systems. from zero.

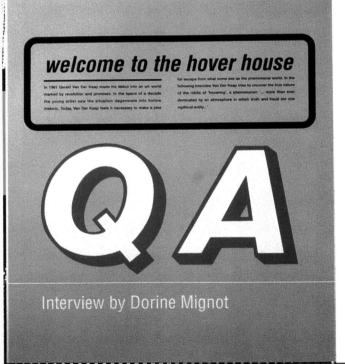

welcome to the hover house

In 1981 Gerald Van Der Kaap made his debut into an art world marked by revolution and promises. In the space of a decade the young artist saw the situation degenerate into hollow rhetoric. Today, Van Der Kaap feels it necessary to make a plea for escape from what some see as the phenomenal world. In the following interview Van Der Kaap tries to uncover the true nature of the riddle of 'hovering', a phenomenon '... more than ever dominated by an atmosphere in which truth and fraud are one mythical entity...'

QA

Interview by Dorine Mignot

QUESTION

What prompted you to create **'FREE'**? It's a very symbolic opening to the exhibition.

*) The composition of the exhibition in the museum is based on four key works each of which is displayed in a cabinet. 'FREE' is the title of one of these works. An imaginary exhibition – existing only in print – runs parallel with the real thing (see pages 06-13 for installation views). According to Van Der Kaap this makes the second, parallel exhibition, public domain by definition. 'hover hover is free'. Asked for a possible link between the two he says: They both exist. Any relationship is arbitrary but that in no way affects their validity.

ANSWER

The inspiration was a blonde. It's fall 1989 and I'm taking the train back from installing an exhibition in Southern Germany. This blonde starts talking to me in the restaurant car. Maybe she was wearing a blond wig, they all do nowadays. She suggested that we eat dinner together. While we're eating I tell about my plan to travel around the world – in however-many-days.[1] And about my reluctance to actually make a start. She fucks her blouse more tightly in her skirt, like real cool, and starts to tell me about a recent inheritance, the complete archives of a German documentary photographer. The guy – I forget his name – had travelled around the world making independent photo documentaries, early this century. She had a whole range on subjects in these archives: Mussolini and his environment, African landscapes, horses, labourers and – naturally – a whole bunch of blondes. But one photo intrigued her especially: a shot of his bag containing everything you needed then for travel photography. You could not travel without a bag like this (.) At that time I also published the principles for this journey around the world, in which I described a theory of the carnivalesque.[2]

① *however-many-days: Van Der Kaap recently described the journey at 'The New Concept' symposium in Graz, Austria; he declared that the journey would be 'an ironic Odyssey, situated in the world's financial centers, recording them in photographic images, as a monument, as highlight, just as every culture, including our own, deserves. A grand and compelling monument, and at the same time a caricature of itself. The subject calls for an image that is at once specific and general: specific in the sense that everything can be related to the manifestation of culture, commerce and power, and their revelation (these we can take with us in the form of photographs of bank buildings, brothels, monuments, means of transport, alleyways, works of art, women of all nations...); general in the striving towards the one imaginary city linked by satellites.'*

The photographs to be taken will be published in book form: 'A book of photographs, in the classic sense, but placed in a different tradition, a 'carnivalesque' tradition. It will be a reversal of the genre of photojournalism. The form will be artificially borrowed from documentary photography, without the laws of motivation and involvement associated with it. The story as a pornographic poem of power'.

Regarding method, Van Der Kaap wrote:

> The polish of an ad photographer. The malice of a paparazzo.

② *a theory of the carnivalesque: Van Der Kaap got the idea after reading an article entitled 'On the carnivalesque': 'The carnivalesque represents the transposition into culture of the spirit of carnival. The carnivalesque principle abolishes hierarchies, levels social classes and artistic genres. In carnival, all that is marginalized and excluded – the mad, the scandalous, the aleatory – takes over the centre in a liberating explosion of 'otherness'. It is a symbolic defeat over death, over all that is sacred, over all that oppresses and restricts.'*

montage van de foto's met toevoeging van geluid en muziek en laten wij het populair zeggen 'commentaar', voldoet mij niet [...] Maar ik geloof dat er tussen de fotografie, tv en film nog wel een 'nieuw' gebied af te bakenen valt, waarin meer dan in één van de genoemde media een bepaald accent gelegd kan worden, met gebruikmaking van zekere elementen uit de betreffende media.[17]

Nadat er aan het eind jaren zestig en het begin van de jaren zeventig enkele goedkoop uitgevoerde foto- boeken met een actie-achtige opmaak waren gemaakt, werd in de loop van de jaren zeventig de vormgeving van fotoboeken rustiger. Foto's kregen steeds meer de behandeling van autonome kunstwerken met eigen esthetische kwaliteiten. Deze ontwikkeling laat zich goed illustreren aan de hand van de fotoboeken **Frimangron** (1975) en **the Dutch Caribbean** (1978) die Willem Diepraam in samenwerking met de journalist Gerard van Westerloo en grafisch vormgever Jan van Toorn over Suriname en de Nederlandse Antillen maakte. Frimangron was door Van Toorn sterk vanuit de inhoud opgemaakt. Hij had de foto's, vaak klein van formaat, en de tekst als gelijkwaardige informatie- dragers samengevoegd, om zo de verwarde realiteit van Suriname aan de vooravond van haar onafhankelijkheid te tonen.

In zijn typografie streeft Van Toorn naar een *open vormstructuur* waardoor de beschouwer wordt aangezet tot reflectie en tot het vormen van een eigen mening. Zo stelde hij: Ik zoek voortdurend naar een structuur om de chaos te beheersen en te ordenen, maar ik keer de gevonden ordening ogenblikkelijk om ten gunste van de chaos. Onze beleving van de werkelijkheid verarmt, wanneer alles geordend en te verifiëren zou zijn. Chaos is een essentieel gegeven, dat ons voortdurend herinnert aan een irrationele, emotionele en moeilijk met verbale middelen aan te duiden werkelijkheidsbeleving. Ik beschouw het als mijn taak om met visuele middelen dit spanningsveld inzichtelijk te maken.[18]

In Frimangron zijn veel reportages van Diepraam opgenomen over religieuze uitingen van de diverse bevolkingsgroepen in Suriname. De foto's van Javaanse dansers in trance, bezeten door een paardengeest, geven een indruk van de voor ons westerlingen moeilijk te begrijpen Voodoo-praktijken binnen het Moslimgeloof. Zij vormen het *chaotische element* in de lay-out van Van Toorn. In de direct naast de foto's geplaatste tekst beschrijft Van Westerloo deze mysterieuze uitingen, en tracht er een verklaring voor te geven. De tekst brengt de *ordening* aan. The Dutch Caribbean kende een geheel andere opzet. In overleg met Diepraam had Van Toorn het fotodeel en het tekstdeel van elkaar gescheiden, en bijna alle foto's in groot formaat op afzonderlijke pagina's aangebracht. Het ging nu, ondanks de journalistieke benadering van Van Westerloo niet

17 Inleiding uit ongepubliceerd scenario *Les Amoureux*, p. 2. Zie C. van der Harten, *Sanne Sannes fotograaf* (ongepubliceerde doctoraalscriptie kunstgeschiedenis), Rijksuniversiteit Utrecht 1988.

17 Introduction to the unpublished scenario, *Les Amoureux*, p. 2. See C. van der Harten, *Sanne Sannes fotograaf* (unpublished Ph.D. thesis in art history), Rijksuniversiteit Utrecht 1988

18 E. Rodrigo, 'Evert Rodrigo over Jan van Toorn', *Openbaar Kunstbezit* 30(1986)2 ('Grafisch vormgevers en beeldende kunst'), p. 59.

18 E. Rodrigo, 'Evert Rodrigo on Jan van Toorn', *Openbaar Kunstbezit* 30 (1986)2 ('Graphic designers and the visual arts'), p. 59.

goal was to make a film-novel in photographs. Sannes wrote: I am never satisfied simply with a projection of photographs plus a sound track and music and, to use the popular expression, a 'commentary' doesn't satisfy me [...] But I believe that between photography, TV and film there is a new territory to be explored, in which, more than in any one of these media by itself, some specific things can be highlighted by using certain elements from the media concerned'.[17]

At the end of the Sixties and the beginning of the Seventies a number of cheaply produced photobooks with an action-like layout were made. However, as the Seventies continued the design of photobooks became more restful. Photographs were treated increasingly as autonomous works of art with their own aesthetic qualities. This development is well illustrated by photobooks such as **Frimangron** (1975) and **The Dutch Caribbean** (1978) that Willem Diepraam made about Surinam (Dutch Guyana) and the Dutch Antilles in collaboration with the journalist Gerard van Westerloo and the graphic designer Jan van Toorn. Van Toorn's layout for Frimangron relied pronouncedly on the content of the book. He combined text and photo- graphs, often in a small format, as information carriers with equal status, with the aim of showing the confused reality of Surinam on the eve of its independence.

In his typography Van Toorn aimed at an *open design structure* the purpose of which was to stimulate the viewer to reflection and to making up his own mind about what he was viewing. Because, as he said: I am constantly in search of a structure in order to control chaos and put some order into it, but I immediately overturn the order I've found in favour of chaos. Our experience of reality becomes impoverished when everything is in its place and can be verified. Chaos is an essential fact. We are constantly reminded of the existence of an irrational, and emotional experience of reality that is difficult to express in words. I see it as my task to provide insight into this field of tension with visual means.[18]

Frimangron contains many reports by Diepraam about the religious rituals of different groups of the population in Surinam. The photographs of Javanese dancers in a state of trance, possessed by the spirit of a horse, give an impression of Voodoo practices within Islam that are difficult for us Westerners to comprehend. This is the *chaotic element* in Van Toorn's layout. In the text, placed directly next to the photographs, Van Westerloo describes these mysterious manifestations, and attempts to explain them. The text provides the element of *order*. The Dutch Caribbean has a completely different layout. After discussing the matter with Diepraam, Van Toorn kept the photographs and the textual part of the book

76

Sex a Gogo van Sanne Sannes verscheen in 1969 postuum. Vormgever Walter Steevensz knipte in de foto's en maakte gebruik van teksten voor een speelse, 'pop-art'-achtige opbouw van het boek.

Sex a Gogo by Sanne Sannes appeared posthumously in 1969. The designer Walter Steevensz cut the photographs and used text to give the book a cheerful 'pop-art' look.

Sahel (1982) by Willem Diepraam was designed in a very calm way by Jan van Toorn. The typography of the title page of the book was placed in such a way that it suggests the heat of the Sahel. A double page from the retro- spective book Parijs 1950-1954! by Ed van der Elsken laid out in a filmic way by Anthon Beeke in 1981.

FRED STRUVING

The book *Photographs between Covers* (1989), designed by Fred Struving and printed by Mart. Spruijt, explores the structure of the traditional typographic book. The designer has used the center of the page as a channel for citational notes and as a space into which quotations are indented. Like many Dutch publications, it is bi-lingual; the Dutch marginalia is set flush-left; the English is flush-right. A frieze across the bottom holds images.

HENRIK BARENDS
As director of an Amsterdam design studio called
The Baudelaire Group,
Henrik Barends has
developed an insistently
individualistic style. Since
1985, Barends has used
computers to manipulate
typographic form, often
pushing his designs over the
brink of legibility.
His distorted letters serve—
at the very least—
as instantly recognizable
logotypes for Barends' own
style, as in this cover and
title page for a book on
Dutch typography, 1990.

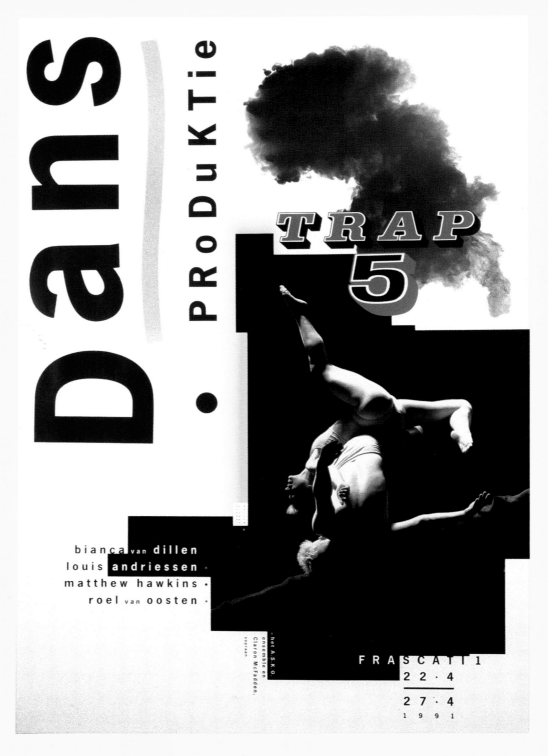

JACQUES KOEWEIDEN *and* PAUL POSTMA
Since forming their Amsterdam-based partnership in 1986, Koeweiden and Postma have received numerous awards for their posters and house styles. The dance posters shown here combine modernist compositional devices with unusual display typography and discordant interruptions in the texts and images. Koeweiden and Postma are both graduates of the Royal Academy of Art and Design, 1983 and 1984 respectively.

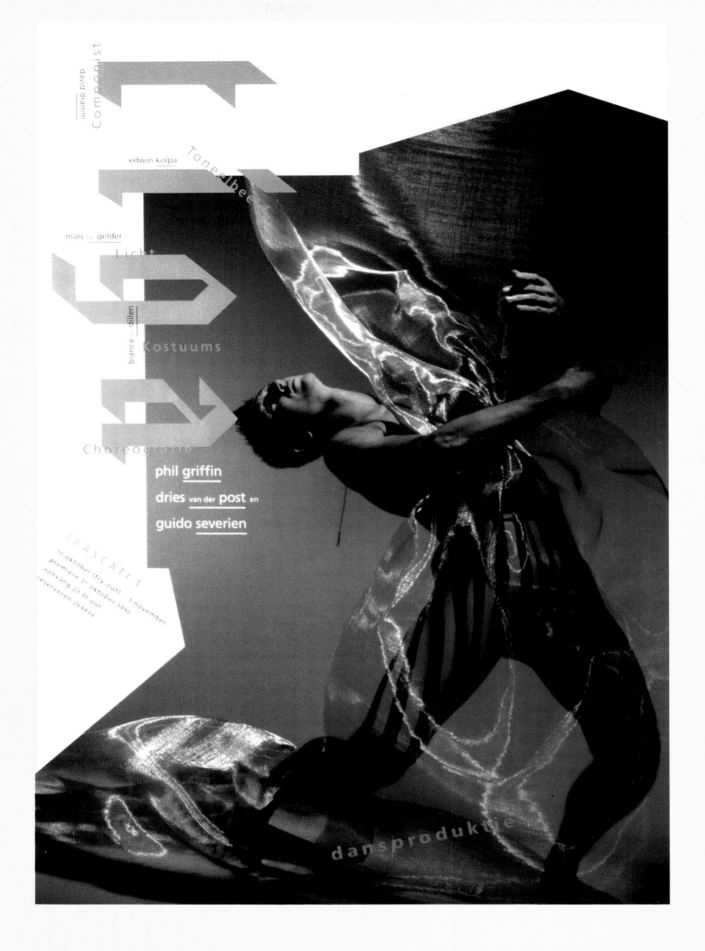

Componist
david dramm

Toneelbeeld
edwin kolpa

Licht
marc de gelder

Kostuums
bianca dillen

Choreografie
phil griffin
dries van der post en
guido severien

FRASCATI 1
10 oktober (try out) – 1 november
premiere 31 oktober 1990
aanvang 20.30 uur
reserveren 266866

dansproduktie

REYNOUD HOMAN

Located in an industrial section of Amsterdam, the office of Reynoud Homan produces books, posters, annual reports, and house styles for a diverse clientele. Homan, who worked for Total Design in the late 70s, remains committed to a modernist methodology. He is interested in graphic design as an "industrial product"—he thus loves to study the processes of printing and manufacture. He explains, "To discover the limits of a technical project is the sport of graphic design." The cover of the book ABOVE (1989) is made of 5/8"-thick cardboard—as heavy as the binding machine would allow.

While Homan is a highly skilled typographic designer, the books at right use images *in place of* words. ABOVE is a page from the catalogue of a ceramics exhibition; the curving tonality of the book merges with the soft gradations of the full-bleed photograph. BELOW is a page from a publication produced in connection with a corporate art commission. The book includes almost no words; Homan has paired each photograph of the artist's work with a small, schematic icon— a zero-degree visual text. Homan studied at the Koninklijke Academy in The Hague and at the University of Reading, Great Britain.

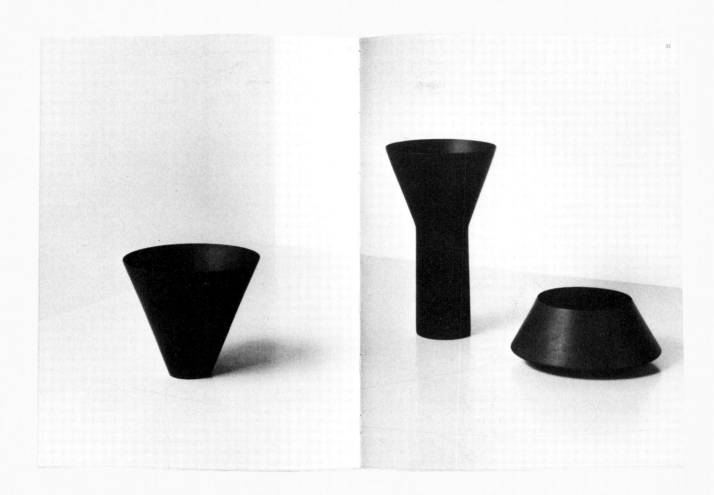

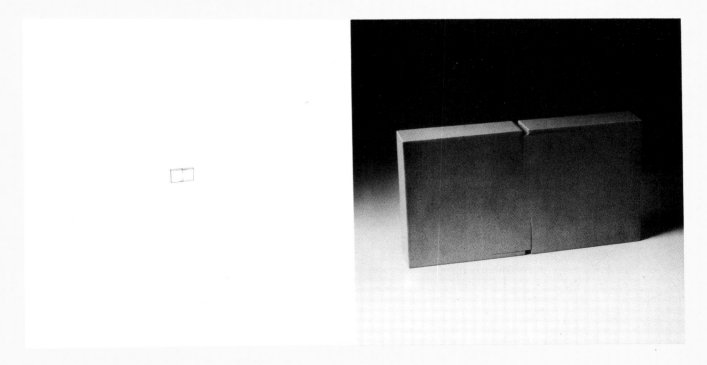

COMPOSITIE MET ROZEN

Processen van beeldvorming in het werk van

Paul Beckman
Daan van Golden
Charlie van Rest
Joop Schafthuizen

MART WARMERDAM

Since graduating from the Rietveld Academy in 1986, Mart Warmerdam has been a free lance designer in Amsterdam. His office is located in the same cavernous industrial warehouse as Reynoud Homan. Like Homan, Warmerdam is interested in the book as a physical object. ABOVE are covers of exhibition catalogues that present the surface of the book as a continuous visual field: typography is treated as a secondary element. The book at RIGHT is a collection of student architectural proposals; its pages are bound with a central rivet.

Micro Meso Macro Zoals het begrip Kunstenplan inmiddels is ingeburgerd, zo zullen ook de termen micro, meso en macro steeds vertrouwder gaan klinken. Het komt al steeds vaker voor dat binnen de Raad gesproken wordt over de advisering op micro-, meso- en macroniveau. Met microniveau wordt dan de ad hoc-advisering over projecten en manifestaties bedoeld, met mesoniveau de advisering over structurele en meerjarige subsidievertrekkingen aan instellingen en gezelschappen en met macroniveau de al dan niet sectorgebonden beleidsadvisering. De termen micro, meso en macro stammen dan wel uit het Grieks, maar ze zijn kort en bondig, liggen goed op de tong en in het gehoor. Als ik het Grieks woordenboek er niet op nageslagen had, zou ik zelfs jou er durven gaan om een raadslid met een bepaalde deskundigheid als een typische microman of mesovrouw te omschrijven. Maar ik heb de Griekse dictionaire wel geraadpleegd. En dat heeft me op dat punt toch wat terughoudend gemaakt. Wat betekent micros? Niet alleen klein en kort – betekenissen die goed van pas komen –, maar ook gering, onbeduidend en onaanzienlijk. Arme incidentele projecten! Slaan we het woordenboek bij mesos open, dan staat er precies wat we bedoelen nl. midden, zich in het midden bevindend. Maar daar blijft het niet bij. Mesos betekent ook middelmatig, matig en weinig. Zo'n benaming kan je (toneel)gezelschappen uit onze vocabulaire? Laat ik nog een kleine exercitie maken alvorens te besluiten. Voordat micro, meso en macro in zwang raakten, onderscheidde de Raad twee soorten advisering: de beleidsadvisering en de concrete advisering. Met beleidsadvisering werden de adviezen aangeduid die de betrekking hadden op bijvoorbeeld het dansbestel of het opdrachtenbeleid. Op concrete advisering sloeg alles wat de Raad daarnaast deed. En dat was vooral adviezen uitbrengen over al die honderden projecten en manifestaties. Ook de adviezen over bijvoorbeeld de dans- en toneelgezelschappen behoorden daarbij. Die waren zozeer in de minderheid dat ze gewoon bij concreet werden ingedeeld. Door de invoering van het vierjaarlijkse Kunstenplan is de indeling in beleidsadvisering en concrete advisering niet meer geschikt. In het Kunstenplan staan de instellingen en gezelschappen centraal, ruim 170 in getal. Die moeten voortaan allemaal jaarlijks door de Raad worden gevolgd; iedere vier jaar moet er een advies over uitgebracht. Dat is nieuw, in ieder geval voor de meeste sectoren. Voor deze instellingen en gezelschappen, verdeeld over de subsidie-categorieën structureel en meerjarig, is eveneens aandacht gewenst. Die waren tot nu toe vooral een zaak van de afdeling en niet van de Raad in zijn geheel. Of ook: de instellingen en gezelschappen waar het hier om gaat, zijn het middelpunt, de spil, de infrastructuur van het kunstbeleid. Zonder hen zou het kunstbeleid als een pudding in elkaar zakken. Zoiets. De term concrete advisering voldoet niet meer, omdat zij projecten en instituten over dezelfde kam scheert. Er is behoefte aan een duidelijk onderscheid. Niet alleen de Raad is op zoek naar een duidelijk beeld van de soorten advisering, ook de Minister van wvc doet pogingen helderheid te scheppen. Zo bericht hij de Tweede Kamer in zijn nota naar aanleiding van het eindverslag over het voorstel van Wet houdende wijziging van de Wet op de Raad voor de Kunst 1977 dat er in de advisering over artistieke keuzevraagstukken en over kunstbeleid maar liefst vier niveaus zijn te onderscheiden. Dit niet in termen van hiërarchie, zo schrijft de Minister, 'maar in termen van het onderscheid tussen meer specifiek en meer algemeen. Op het eerste niveau gaat het om beoordeling, afweging, prioriteitstelling binnen één kunstvorm, binnen één artistieke discipline, bijvoorbeeld die van het poppenspel. Vervolgens komt het niveau waarop de sector aan de orde, bijvoorbeeld het theater. Daarna het niveau waarop de verschillende sectoren en kunstvormen over de grenzen van disciplines heen onderling worden vergeleken. Zoals in het geval van de kunstenbrief. Tenslotte is er het niveau waar het gaat om de positie van de kunsten midden in de andere sectoren van het cultuurbeleid, het cultuurbeleid in relatie tot... etc.' Vier niveaus, terwijl binnen de Raad aan drie niveaus wordt gedacht. Bovendien hecht de Raad een andere betekenis aan de niveaus 1 en 2. Recentelijk zijn de profielschetsen van de afdelingen van de Raad verschenen onder verantwoordelijkheid van de Adviescommissie Benoeming Leden Raad voor de Kunst. Dit om de vacatures binnen het ledenbestand van de Raad onder de aandacht te brengen, die per 1 september 1989 moeten worden vervuld. In die profielschetsen komt een passage voor over de advisering door de Raad. Die luidt als volgt: 'Ten aanzien van de advisering kan onderscheid worden gemaakt tussen adviezen over kwesties die met bepaalde artistieke sectoren verband houden, en adviezen over vraagstukken van meer algemene aard (..). Bij de adviezen die meer op bepaalde artistieke disciplines betrekking hebben, waarbij het soms om beleidsmatige aangelegenheden en doorgaans om (artistieke) keuze-vraagstukken gaat, kunnen verschillende niveaus worden onderscheiden, afhankelijk o.a. van de vraag of de advisering betrekking heeft op één discipline (bijvoorbeeld de mime), een sector (bijvoorbeeld de theatersector) of juist intersectorale, danwel sectoroverstijgende vraagstukken'. Bij de adviezen over vraagstukken van meer algemene aard kan gedacht worden aan adviezen inzake de wetgeving op het terrein van het kunst- en cultuurbeleid, de inrichting van het hoger kunstonderwijs en de positie van vrouwen op het terrein van de cultuur. Tot dit gebied behoort ook de aandacht die volgt uit de creatie van een niveau 1, dat de instellingen en gezelschappen omvat en niet primair is toegespitst op het maken van keuzes binnen één sector zoals Minister en Adviescommissie het voorstellen. Wat zij bedoelen, is veeleer een beleidsafweging die echter op een andere wijze zichtbaar moet worden gemaakt. Als we het nu eens zo zien: niveau 1 vormt de advisering over projecten, niveau 2 over de instituten, niveau 3 vormt de beleidsadvisering met het volgende onderscheid: a) binnen een sector, b) tussen sectoren onderling (à la kunstenbrief) en c) in algemene zin. Dan zijn we er toch uit? En kunnen we voor de niveaus 1, 2 en 3 nu voortaan de termen micro, meso en macro hanteren of laten we ons door het Griekse woordenboek hiervan weerhouden? Ik stel voor ook op dit vlak enig risico te nemen. In de jaren negentig zal de klok micro, meso en macro slaan. Yvonne van Baarle, algemeen secretaris 4

Evenals voorgaande jaren kwam de Raad voor de Kunst in het verslagjaar éénmaal in plenaire vergadering bijeen. Deze gebeurtenis vond plaats op 14 oktober in de Aula van het Haags Gemeentemuseum. Professor dr M.P.C.M. van Schendelen, hoogleraar politicologie aan de Erasmus Universiteit Rotterdam, hield in aansluiting op de huishoudelijke vergadering een inleiding over het onderwerp: 'Omgaan met de politiek'. Het onderwerp 'lobbyen' kwam in dit kader uitgebreid aan de orde. Bij de installatie van de nieuwe leden van de Raad en het afscheid van de leden die de Raad per 1 september verlieten, hield de Minister van Welzijn, Volksgezondheid en Cultuur, mr drs L.C. Brinkman, een toespraak. De Minister memoreerde de gang van zaken rond de vaststelling van het Kunstenplan. Hij constateerde dat de Tweede Kamer hierin de meest bepalende rol heeft gespeeld en wees de aanwezigen erop dat dit is zoals het hoort te zijn. De Minister ziet een taakverschuiving voor de Raad voor de Kunst in het verschiet. Nu het kunstenbeleid meer vanuit algemene beleidsnoties ontwikkeld zal worden, zal de Raad voor de Kunst in staat moeten zijn meer te adviseren vanuit algemenere noties. Weliswaar juicht de Minister het toe wanneer de Raad zich politiek actiever zou opstellen (met bijbehorende lobby-activiteiten), maar hij is geen belangenorganisatie. De Raad behartigt het belang van 'de kunsten'. Op dit terrein staat, in de opvatting van de Minister, de Raad vooral voor de taak respect af te dwingen door op bevlogen wijze op grond van artistiek-inhoudelijke oordelen zorg te dragen voor het kwalitatieve aspect in de oordeelsvorming. De tekst van de rede van mr drs L.C. Brinkman, Minister van Welzijn, Volksgezondheid en Cultuur, is gepubliceerd in IB 1988, nr. 6. 5

IRMA BOOM produces complex yet classical work characterized by an exacting attention to typographic detail, a fascination with the physical processes of printing and book-binding, and a commitment to the purity of her concepts that sometimes allows her to sacrifice standards of legibility in order to preserve the integrity of an idea—she has been known, for example, to use excruciatingly long line lengths. ABOVE is the annual report for a government art commission (1988); this strictly typographic book is printed in red, yellow, and blue ink, resulting in brownish black type, with pure colors used for emphasis. BELOW is Boom's book commemorating the PTT's stamp designs (1988); the folded leaves have been bound but not cut—thus pictures printed on the hidden interior of the folded pages show through on the exposed reading surfaces: mysterious shadows are cast on the text from *inside* the book.

TON VAN BRAGT

Now an independent designer, Ton van Bragt worked for Studio
Dumbar from 1985 to 1991, after graduating from the St. Joost
Academy in Breda. The pages shown ABOVE are from a booklet for a
cultural festival. The larger sheet of paper on which the booklet was
printed has a poster on one side (shown at RIGHT), and the festival
program on the other. When cut down and bound as a book,
segments of the poster function as abstract, randomly generated
illustrations. The result is brilliantly economical.

Francisco Ulloa Dominicaanse Republiek
La Charanga de Paris Dominicaanse Rep./Frankrijk
Fuzué Nederland/Brazilie
Coupe Cubana Nederland
Dansorgel De Cubaan Nederland
Kopro Toe Gelegenheidsformatie

Nighttown Rotterdam, Kruiskade 28 NIGHTTOWN
Aanvang 20.30 uur (Zaal open 19.30 uur)
Toegang fl 30,- (Voorverkoop fl 25,-)

AFRO
CARIBE

NIGHTTOWN

1991

VRIJDAG 20 SEPT.

Vincent van Baar
Currently working independently in The Hague,
Vincent van Baar formerly worked for Studio Dumbar;
his designs there include the logo for Zee Belt Theater
(LEFT) and the publication Zee Zucht (ABOVE).
The logos play on the doubling of vowels characteristic
of Dutch spelling—Van Baar has added spurious
cross bars to the letter *e*. Cover image designed by Gert
Dumbar; photography by Lex van Pieterson.
Van Baar is a graduate of St. Joost Academy in Breda.

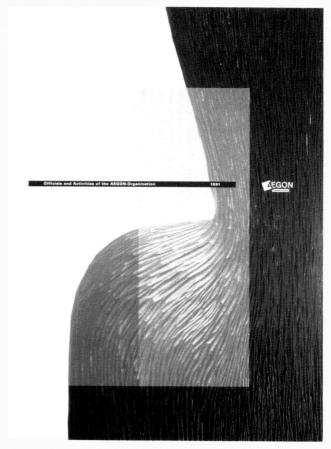

HARMINE LOUWÉ

Several talented designers are currently on staff
at Studio Dumbar; among them is Harmine Louwé.
Under the charismatic leadership of Gert Dumbar,
the studio has allowed her and others to develop their
own unique design styles, often for corporate clients,
as in this pair of publications for Aegon, an insurance
company. The work of Louwé is painterly and
abstract; her organic forms range from the elegantly
arabesque (see p.2) to the viscerally organic. Louwé
is a graduate of St. Joost Academy.

The Authors

WILLIAM DEERE is Assistant Professor of Design at State University of New York, Purchase; he has also taught at North Carolina State University and University of Michigan, Ann Arbor. He has an MFA in graphic design from the Cranbrook Academy of Art. In 1986 he was a *stagiaire* at Studio Dumbar.

ROBIN KINROSS is a typographer and publisher in London. He has written widely on design, for publications including *Eye, Information Design Journal, Journal of Design History,* and *Design Issues.* His book *Modern Typography: An Essay in Critical History* is forthcoming, 1992.

DAAN DE KUYPER is a Dutch art historian. She was the former graphic design co-ordinator for the Centraal Museum in Utrecht, The Netherlands. She currently lives and works in New York.

ELLEN LUPTON has been curator of the Herb Lubalin Study Center since it opened in 1985. As of March 1992, she will be Curator of Contemporary Design at the Cooper-Hewitt, National Museum of Design. She has written for publications including *Eye, Print, Design Issues,* and *AIGA Journal of Graphic Design.*

MONICA STRAUSS is the proprietor of MJS Books and Graphics, New York, specializing in early twentieth-century avant-garde printed ephemera. She has a Ph.D. in art history from the Institute of Fine Arts, NYU. She has taught at Brooklyn College, NYU, and the Cooper-Hewitt Museum's MA program in the Decorative Arts. She writes for *Fine Print.*

Resources

"The Dutch Issue." Special issue of *Print* XLV:VI (November/December 1991). Includes essays on historical and contemporary commercial design.

"Printing Arts in the Netherlands." Special issue of *Fine Print* Vol. 15 No. 4 (October 1989). Includes essays on historical and contemporary book arts.

Holland in Vorm: Dutch Design 1945-1987. Ed. Gert Staal and Hester Wolters. Amsterdam: Stichting Holland in Vorm, 1987. Includes chapters on architecture, product design, graphic design, jewelry, and more. Text in English.

Typographie Hollandaise. Catalogue for an exhibition held at the Maison du Livre de l'Image et du Son, Villeurbanne, France, 1991. Text in French and English.

Typofoto: Elementaire Typographie in Nederland, 1920-40. Dick Mann and John van Der Ree. Utrecht and Antwerpen: Reflex, 1990. Illustrated account of avant-garde graphic design in Holland. Text in Dutch.

Wabnitz Editions

For people interested in collecting contemporary Dutch design, Wabnitz Editions offers a subscription service which delivers to its members a selection of fifteen recent Dutch posters every six months, along with the quarterly magazine *Affiche/Poster.* Included are posters for theaters, museums, festivals, and other cultural concerns, as well as quality printed advertising.

For more information, contact
Wabnitz Editions
P.O. Box 30117
6803 AC Arnhem
The Netherlands